Messerschmitt Bf 109

in action

Part 2

by John R. Beaman, Jr.
illustrated by Don Greer

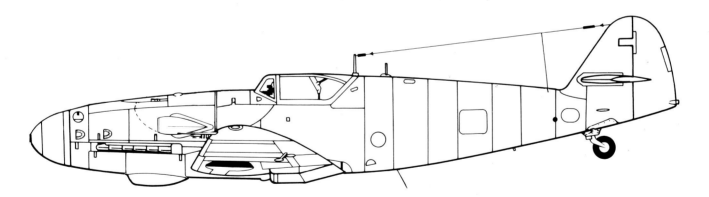

Aircraft Number 57
squadron/signal publications

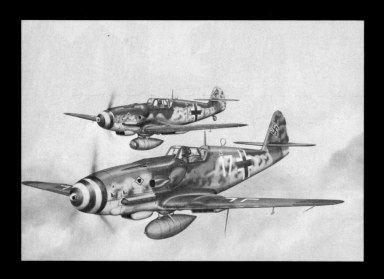

Two aircraft from JG 53 and JG 77 join up for a long flight back to Germany from the Ardennes in late December 1944.

ISBN 0-89747-138-5

If you have any photographs of the aircraft, armor, soldiers or ships of any nation, particularly wartime snapshots, why not share them with us and help make Squadron/Signal's books all the more interesting and complete in the future. Any photograph sent to us will be copied and the original returned. The donor will be fully credited for any photos used. Please send them to: Squadron/Signal Publications, Inc., 1115 Crowley Dr., Carrollton, TX 75011-5010.

Photo Credits

Gene Stafford	I.W.M.
Hans Obert	Hans Rossbach
E.C.P. Armee	Steve Cook
Michael Pruett	USAF
U.S. Archives	Frantisek Sazel
Bundes Archiv	Zdenek Titz
Smithsonian	James Crow
Jean Cuny	

Dedicated to Steve Cook
who inspired a lifetime passion

William Green has pointed out that...

A vital attribute of any successful combat aircraft design is a capacity for development, for, without such, it cannot hope to keep pace for long with the changing demands and fluctuations of aerial warfare. Such a quality, provided it demands no extensive redesign of fundamental components with consequent major retooling, can be of incalculable value.

During the early spring of 1940, well before the Battle of France began, the Messerschmitt design team at Augsburg set about updating and refining their progeny. Designed to take full advantage of the more powerful 1350HP DB 601E engine the resultant Bf 109F series has been claimed by many to have carried Messerschmitt's fighter to the "crest of its evolution".

Using standard Bf 109E-4 air frames, Werk-Nrs 5601-5604, four prototypes, V21, V22, V23 and V24 respectively were built to test various aerodynamic and powerplant revisions. The F was designed as an exercise in lessening air drag beginning with a completely new cowling designed to enclose the DB 601E engine and with a slightly deeper oil cooler bath underneath the cowling. The new round supercharger air intake was moved further out from the side of the cowling to obtain a greater ramming effect. The spinner was considerably enlarged and rounded while the propeller blades were shortened from 10FT 2IN to 9FT 8½IN. The wing mounted MG FF cannon were deleted in favor of a single, engine-mounted Mauser MG 151 firing through an aperture in the spinner. This weapon not only had a higher muzzle velocity and rate of fire than the MG FF but was being developed in both a 15MM and 20MM version.

The wing which had remained essentially the same since the prototype, was structurely unchanged. The underwing radiator was streamlined, being flatter but wider for less drag, providing an air discharge through a duct in the upper portion of the inboard flap which was split length-wise to form a double flap, the radiators were also enlarged horizontally thus providing the same amount of cooling area. The wing leading edge slots were reduced in length as were the flaps which were increased in chord so that their area remained unchanged. The wingspan was reduced, but because of the detrimental effect on handling, detachable semi-ellipitcal wing tips were added.

The size of the rudder was reduced from an area of 8.1 to 7.5 SQ. FT with the symetrical fin being replaced by a cambered one. The bracing struts on the tailplane were deleted and the tailplane was placed slightly below and forward of its position on the E series. The tail wheel was made semi-retractable and six degrees of forward rake was added to the main landing gear in order to slightly lower the ground position of the nose during take off.

Bf 109 E-4

Bf 109 F-0

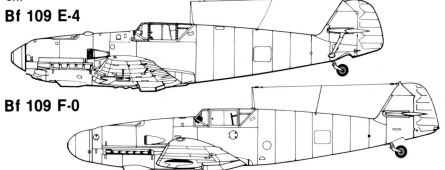

Ten Bf 109F-0 preproduction prototypes were ordered, but neither the DB 601E engine nor the MG 151 cannon were available when these left the assembly line during late fall of 1940. Powered by a DB 601N engine and armed with an engine mounted MG FF/M cannon and a pair of cowl mounted MG 17s and still with the E-type supercharger intake, the Bf 109F-0 received glowing reports from service evaluation units. Evaluated against a similiarly powered Bf 109E-4/N the redesigned machine proved to be considerably more maneuverable, it could both turn inside the E-4/N and climb faster, and while some pilots questioned the adequacy of the three gun configuration, overall marks for the new fighter were extremely high. "Messerschmitt had done it again".

Developmental Drawings

Bf 109 F-1

Bf 109 F-2

Bf 109 F-2z/Trop

Bf 109 F-4

Bf 109 F-4/z

Bf 109 F-6

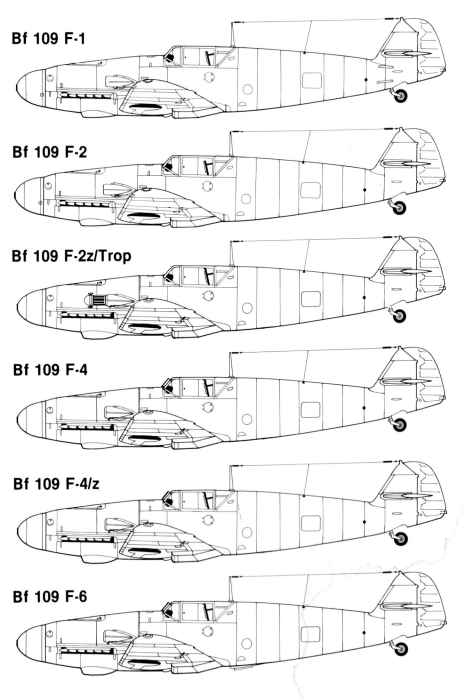

Bf 109F-1

While the Luftwaffe was still evaluating the Bf 109F-0 preproduction aircraft during the late fall of 1940, assembly was begun on the first batch of Bf 109F-1 production aircraft, with delivery to service evaluation units taking place before the end of the year. Since the MG 151 cannon and the DB 601E engine were still not available, the F-1 was essentially the same as the F-0 with the exception that the rectangular supercharger intake was replaced by a new round one.

During February three Bf 109F-1s crashed in unexplained circumstances killing their test pilots. Since two of the pilots had radioed that they were experiencing violent vibrations from the engine just before their aircraft crashed, the DB 601N engine was suspect and immediately all Bf 109Fs were grounded. However since the cause of the vibrations could not be ascertained and no similar accidents were experienced in the like powered Bf 109E-4/N, the ban was lifted. Within weeks another F crashed after losing its tail. Investigation of the crash revealed only superficial damage to the engine, but nearly all of the rivets in the skin plating of the separated tail assembly had broken loose, and many rivets were missing. Investigators quickly found that the unbraced tail, at certain rpms, was subject to a high-frequency oscillation, which was overlapped by the engine vibration which set up sympathetic vibrations, which in turn caused a structural failure. Two external stiffener plates were added to the rear of each side of the fuselage, solving the problem. Service deliveries were resumed, with JG 2 *Richthofen* and JG 26 *Schlageter,* on the Channel coast, being the first recipients during March and April 1941.

Production Variants

Bf 109F-1/B Fighter-bomber equipped with an ETC 250 bomb rack for a 250KG (551LB) SC 250 bomb.
Bf 109F-1/Trop fitted with a dust filter but not desert survival equipment. This was not a production, tropicalized aircraft (which was first done with the F-2), but a field modification using Italian-type filters. Very few of these aircraft were modified before a true, tropicalized version of the F-2 was issued.

(Upper Right) The first Bf 109Fs went to JG 2 and JG 26 posted along the channel coast. This machine belonging to III/JG 2 under the command of Hauptmann Hans "Assi" Hahn, is rolled into a camouflaged hanger. The new fighter was truly a study in sleekness, even to the protruding supercharger intake.

Süpercharger Intakes

 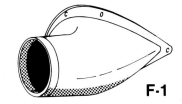

F-0   **F-1**

After the inexplicable crashes were traced to a weakness in the rear fuselage beneath the tail plane, a pair of external stiffeners were added to each side of the aircraft.

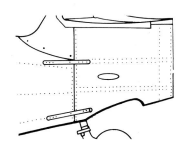

External Stiffeners

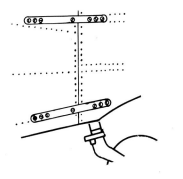

(Above) Just prior to BARBAROSSA, JG 54 was largely re-equipped with F aircraft. This F-1 belongs to the Gruppe Kommodore of II/JG 54 as denoted by the double chevron. The propeller is Black-Green and the colors on the spinner are Yellow circle around gun followed by a thin Red stripe, thin Yellow stripe, wide Red stripe on a Dark Green spinner. In typical JG 54 fashion, the fuselage cross is on a wide Yellow band, and the fuselage sides are a cross-hatch pattern of Black-Green 70, with large splotches of Grau 02.

Tropical Dust Filter

(Open)	(Closed)

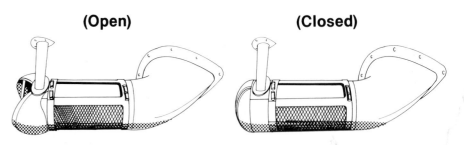

(Above Left) On 10 July 1941, Major Rolf Pingle, a veteran with 26 kills (4 in Spain) and Kommandeur of III/JG 26, was shot down near Dover while chasing a bomber. With only superficial damage his F-1 was repaired and tested by the RAF until it crashed on 20 October when the pilot was overcome by carbon-monoxide fumes. (Gene Stafford)

(Left) Equipped with Bf 109F-1/Bs, 10 (Jabo)/JG 2 carried out hit and run attacks against English targets, tying down large numbers of RAF fighters. Note the Yellow rudder, lower cowling and behing-the-cross chevron and bar, all typical for Jabo aircraft of JG 2.

II/JG 27, equipped with Bf 109F-1 and F-2 aircraft arrived in North Africa in September, 1941. Red 4 is an F-1 carrying the distinctive "Berlin Bear" insignia. The next aircraft and Red 3 appear to be F-2s, one of which has been retrofitted with the armored windscreen glass.

Bf 109F-2

Shortly after the F-1 began reaching operational units along the Channel coast, the faster firing 15MM MG 151/15 cannon was certified for installation in the engine mounting of fighters. Appearing in April 1941, the F-2 was almost identical in appearance to the F-1 except for the engine gun. Early production F-2s still retained the external stiffeners on the rear fuselage. Local internal strengthening however, allowed the deletion of these stiffeners on all but the earliest production F-2 aircraft. Some early production F-1 aircraft had retained the square-shaped wheel wells, in anticipation of wheel well covers that never appeared; all F-2 aircraft had the round well as did the late production F-1 aircraft. The F-2 was produced, at first, simultaneously with the F-1. Priority for re-equipment went to those units in combat on the "Channel Front" such as JG 2, 26, 27 and 53. Units that were earmarked for the Russian campaign were given a somewhat a lower priority, but many were equipped, at least partially with Fs, in time for Operation Barbarossa.

Production Variants

Bf 109F-2/B Fighter-bomber equipped with an ETC 250 bomb rack fro a 250KG (551LB) SC 250 bomb.

Bf 109F-2/Trop fitted with dust filters and desert survival equipment, and a larger supercharger intake like that used later on the Bf 109G.

Bf 109F-2/Z with the GM-1 boost used a VDM propeller with a wider blade, a larger supercharger intake, and a deeper oil cooler under the forward cowling. All these features were subsequently incorporated into the Bf 109G.

(Above Right) A very special F-2: The aircraft of Werner Molders in Russia during the Fall of 1941. The aircraft's spinner, lower cowl, wingtips, fuselage band and rudder are Yellow. The aircraft has been retrofitted with the external windscreen armor and extra pilot armor.

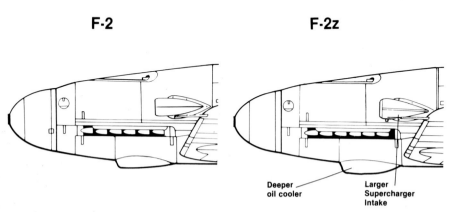

F-2   F-2z

Deeper oil cooler   Larger Supercharger Intake

A rotte of F-2Z/trop aircraft from I/JG 53. The deeper oil cooler of the Z type aircraft is apparent on the nearest aircraft. Note that the lower windscreen panel has been painted over. This is typical for F-2/3/4 aircraft especially in the desert. (Hans Obert)

On December 5, 1941 Reich Marshall Goring visited JG 26. Both of Adolph Galland's specially armed F-2 aircraft were on display. One aircraft, above, had 13MM MG 131 guns mounted in the cowl with small, streamlined bulges on the rear cowl. The front of the bulge can be seem just above the starter crank. (E.C.P. Armees)

(Above Right) A second aircraft had the normal cowl MG-17 guns, but also carried a pair of MG FF cannons in the wings with the E-type installation and lower ammo drum bulge. Galland believed that the F-2 was vastly underarmed for the average pilot's gunnery ability. (E.C.P. Armees)

Adolph Galland's Specially Armed Bf 109 Fs

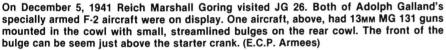

Another view of the wing cannon-armed aircraft. Markings for both aircraft were identical except that Galland's Mickey Mouse insignia faced backwards on the cannon-armed aircraft! The cannon armed aircraft also carried octane triangles calling for 100 octane fuel! (E.C.P. Armees)

Red 9, an F-2/trop being refuelled. In spite of overall dominance by the F equipped Jagflieger units, ground attacks by the RAF made sandbag revetments a necessity of life in the desert.

Yellow 8 of I/JG 27, an F-2/trop, is having its wheel retraction mechanism checked. Notice the large G-type supercharger intake, typical for all F-2/trop aircraft. For some reason the wingtip panel has been removed, affording an excellent view of the wingtip construction. (U.S. Archives)

Gun Barrels

MG 17   MG 131   MG FF 151/15

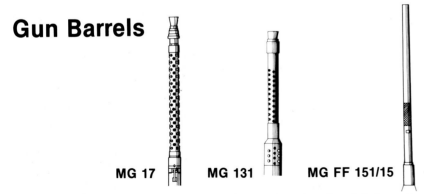

This Bf 109F-2 of IV/JG 51 sits alone on the steppes of southern Russia in late 1941. Note the rarely used IV Gruppe cross symbol, and the White fuselage band and wingtips. This gruppe was eventually broken up to supply replacements for the other three gruppen. (Michael Pruett)

Bf 109F-3

With the DB 601E engine available at last, the production of the F-3 commenced in 1941. In all respects it was visually identical to the F-2 except that the octane triangle now read *87* instead of *C3*. The armament of the F-3 was identical to that of the F-1 with the cowling housing 2 x MG 17 guns and a 20mm MG FF firing through the spinner.

Some sources state that the F-3 was not used operationally, but contemporary evidence indicates that while produced in limited numbers, the F-3 was in fact issued to front-line units, principally JG 2 and JG 26 on the "Channel Front" in 1941/42.

JG 2 and JG 26 faced the tentative probes of the RAF alone, as the bulk of the Jadgruppen moved East for the campaign against Russia. The Jadgflieger of these two units had ample opportunity for action and produced many high-scoring aces. In the upper photo, the F-3 of Joseph "Pips" Priller carries his famous ace of hearts card emblem. Priller commanded 1/JG 26 at the time and later became famous for his lone sortie over the D-Day beaches in 1944.

Octane Triangles

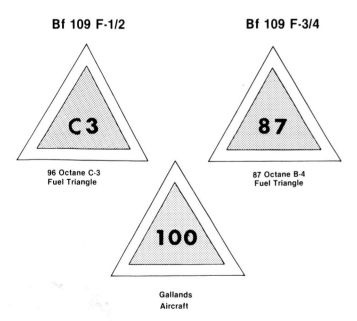

Bf 109 F-1/2

C3

96 Octane C-3
Fuel Triangle

Bf 109 F-3/4

87

87 Octane B-4
Fuel Triangle

100

Gallands
Aircraft

Resplendent in its 76/74/75 camouflage, Yellow 9, the F-3 of Siegfried Schnell sits at dispersal early in 1942. Schnell, Staffel Kapitan of 9/JG 2 at the time, had 57 victories on his Yellow rudder. He was killed in 1944 over Normandy.

Bf 109F-4

With the introduction of the F-4, the *"Friedrick"* series finally reached its development apogee—what it was intended to be from the beginning. It was powered by the powerful DB 601E engine mounting the MG 151/20MM cannon. The pair of cowl mounted MG 17s together with the MG 151 firing through the propeller hub meant a great deal of centrally located fire power, which even a novice pilot could often wield effectively. Pilot protection was increased with the addition of a 6MM armor plate behind and above the pilot's head.

Since the F-series airframe had been designed around the DB 601E powerplant there were few distinguishing differences between the F-4 and its predecessors. The larger supercharger intake of the F-2Z series became standard as did the external armored windscreen which was often retro-fitted to earlier models. The F-4 became the most numerous of all F types and soldiered on until 1943. It was used by virtually every Luftwaffe unit and many Aces were made on the Eastern Front in the F-4. In spite of its relatively short life when compared to the E and the later G series, the F was considered by many to be the best Bf 109 of all, and the F-4 to be the best of the F series.

In order to increase the versatility of the fighter in the field, a series of bolt-on conversion kits were designed that would quickly and easily change the performance of the F-4 to meet local demands. Under the designation *Rustsatze* (field conversion sets), the following were available for the F-4:

R-1 MG 151/20MM cannon under each wing.
R-5 300 liter drop tank under the fuselage.
R-6 ETC 250 bomb rack.

By 1942, the fighter-bomber had become an integral part of each Geschwader and the F-4/B was the most widely used fighter-bomber of the F series. Special units were formed on the Channel coast for hit and run raids against the English coast. These fighter-bomber units of JG 2 and JG 26 were the only ones left in 1941 to harass British defenses since nearly all Luftwaffe bomber units had transferred east or south.

Production Variants

Bf 109F-4/B Fighter-bomber was fitted with various ETC racks to carry bombs, the most popular being the 250KG size.
Bf 109F-4/Trop fitted with dust filters and desert survival equipment including a rifle.
Bf 109F-4/Z equipped with GM-1 boost and using the wider bladed VDM propeller and a deeper oil cooler.

"Blackbirds" at work—groundcrew rearm an F-4 of JG 54 "somewhere in Russia". Clearly shown are the 87 octane markings, the larger supercharger intake, and the thick armored windscreen glass. They are loading 20MM ammunition for the nose MG 151/20. JG 54 used every model of the 109 and fought the entire Eastern Campaign from 1941 to 1945.

Supercharger Intake

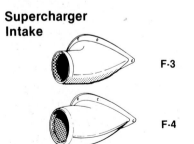

F-3

F-4

External Armored Windscreen

The F-4 introduced increased pilot protection with a 6MM armor plate at a 45° angle to protect the pilot's head. The additional bolt-on armor plate added to the windscreen could be quickly retrofitted to earlier models with only four screws.

This F-4 belonging to the technical officer of III/JG 3 "Udet" carries the Geschwader emblem on the nose and the III Gruppe insignia under the cockpit. The rudder bears five kill marks, the first two of which were claimed on the Western Front. The clump of bushes in the background is actually a heavily camouflaged tent in which the pilots are quartered.

A group of Hungarian Air Force personnel are given a "tour" of this F-4 belonging to II/JG 77. The openess of an airbase on the Russian steppe is well illustrated. Note the parachute on the tailplane, a sign that the unit is likely on alert.

Cockpit Armor

F-3

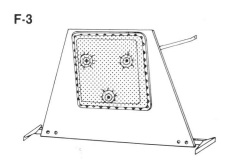

F-4

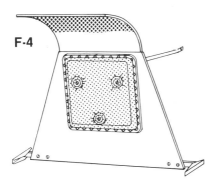

The early spring of 1941 saw the introduction of the Bf 109F-4/Trop into North Africa. This machine, Black 4, carries the Berlin Bear insignia of II/JG 27 just ahead of the dust filter. Just behind the cockpit can clearly be seen the outline of an overpainted N which was part of the factory call sign.

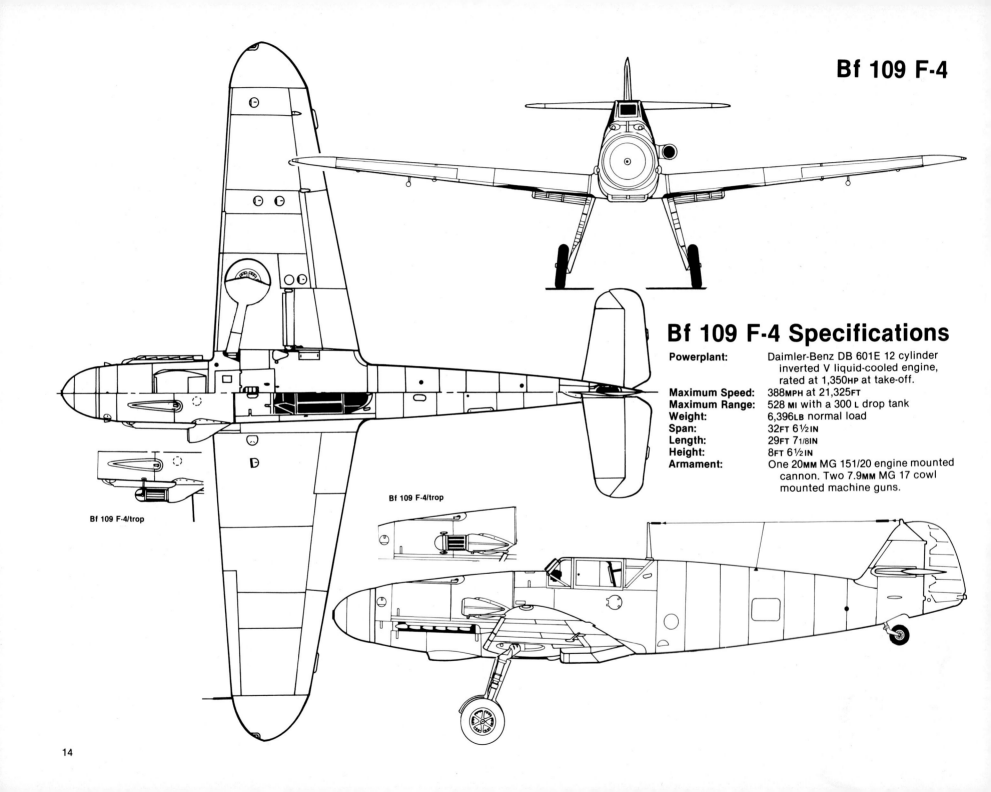

Bf 109 F-4

Bf 109 F-4 Specifications

Powerplant:	Daimler-Benz DB 601E 12 cylinder inverted V liquid-cooled engine, rated at 1,350HP at take-off.
Maximum Speed:	388MPH at 21,325FT
Maximum Range:	528 MI with a 300 L drop tank
Weight:	6,396LB normal load
Span:	32FT 6½IN
Length:	29FT 7 1/8IN
Height:	8FT 6½IN
Armament:	One 20MM MG 151/20 engine mounted cannon. Two 7.9MM MG 17 cowl mounted machine guns.

Bf 109 F-4/trop

Bf 109 F-4/trop

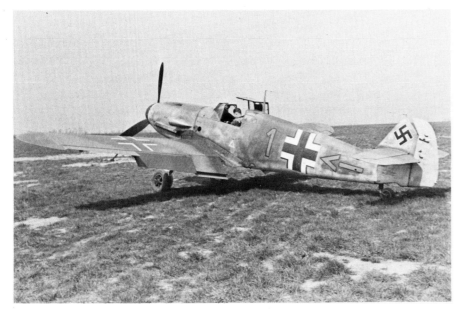

Belonging to the Staffel Kapitan of 10/JG 2, this Bf 109F-4B carries some very unusual markings behind the fuselage Balkenkreuz and some impressive shipping victory marks on it's White rudder.

This F-4, believed to be of I/JG 51 is undergoing a test engine run-up. JG 51 fought on all sectors of the Russian front before being transferred to the Mediterranean in 1942. The camouflage of this aircraft comes unusually far down the fuselage sides. Evidently there's not been time for the ground crew to add a White fuselage band which would complete the theater markings for southern Russia.

Rüstsätze Available for the Bf 109 F-4

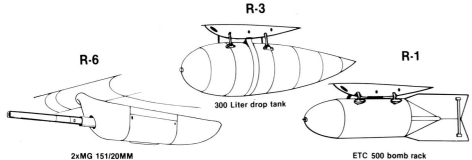

R-3

R-6

R-1

300 Liter drop tank

2xMG 151/20MM

ETC 500 bomb rack

This new F-4/B fighter bomber on the northern sector of the Russian front stands out starkly against the White snow. The Greys that the fighters were delivered in were quickly overpainted with various designs of white distemper during winter months.

Bf 109F-5 and F-6

With its high speed and good altitude performance, the F series was a natural candidate to be developed into a reconnaissance aircraft. It was lacking range so both the F-5 and F-6 carried fuselage racks for the 300 liter drop tank.

The F-5 was a tactical reconnaissance aircraft. As such, it carried the two cowling MG 17 machine guns, but no cameras, photos being supplied by a hand held camera.

The F-6 was the main reconnaissance version of the F series. It was similar to the F-4, but carried only the two MG 17 guns and did not have the external windscreen armored glass. It was equipped in one of three ways: with a Rb 20/30, or Rb 50/30, or the Rb 75/30 camera behind the cockpit with an especially-designed aperture under the fuselage. Although built in limited numbers, the high performance of the F-6 allowed it to stay on operations well into 1943. The G-4 only partially replaced the F-6. There are many documented chases by RAF aircraft over the desert, or over Malta, that never caught what had to be an F-6 doing its job.

A Bf 109F-6 (coded F6 + TH) of 1.(F)/122 simmers in the Sardinian sun of 1942. Note the hand crank for the inertia engine starter and the beach umbrella to keep the cockpit from becoming too hot to touch. The unit spent most of its career in the Mediterranean. Its emblem, on the forward cowling, is a White duck, in flight, over a Red spearpoint. (Smithsonian)

RB 50/30 Camera

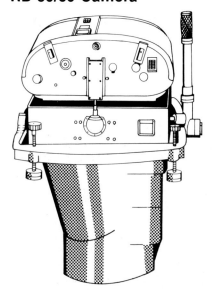

F-6 Camera Installation

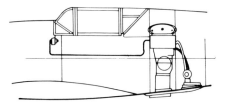

1.(F)/122, a long range reconnaissance unit, operated both Ju88s and Bf 109F-6s from Sardinia during 1942. These F-6/Trops have the deeper oil cooler. (Smithsonian)

Bf 109G "Gustav"

Although the German propaganda mill continued to mouth the cliches of world conquest, by 1941 the *Nazi* leadership had proven itself to be totally incapable of the long-range planning that such a goal required. Indeed, by the summer of 1941 it was becoming increasingly obvious, for those who would look, that the German leadership was incapable of planning and executing even a protracted multi-fronted war that the coming invasion of the Soviet Union would thrust upon the German nation. The Lufwaffe was no exception and, in fact, Udet's *Reichsluftministrium,* which had swollen to some four thousand people, is described by David Irving as being *a rabbit warren of colonels, bureaucrats and engineers, responsible for everything but responsible to nobody.*

Messerschmitt's Bf 109, the backbone of the Luftwaffe fighter force, had reached its pinnacle with production of the F series and as the Luftwaffe began taking delivery of the "Fritz" no successor to the Messerschmitt progeny was on the drawing board. Consequently, during the summer of 1941, as the German juggernaut knifed deep into Russia, the Messerschmitt design team was engaged in yet another update of the now aging Bf 109. Under the designation Bf 109G, or "Gustav" as it affectionately became known among the troops, this version was to become the most numerously produced variant.

Dictates of the air war forced the Messerschmitt design people to sacrifice handling and maneuverability in order to increase maximum speed. Designed around the more powerful but heavier Daimler-Benz DB 605 engine, local strengthening was required which increased weight which, in turn, required that the undercarriage be strengthened which again increased weight; all of which increased wing loading and decreased handling characteristics. The DB 605A powerplant featured an increased cylinder capacity that raised compression to 7.3 in the port cylinder bank and 7.5 in the starboard, increasing rpms to 2800 and horsepower to 1,475 at take off, with no increase in overall engine dimensions. Weight of the new G series escalated to over 6500 LBS, but the RLM felt that, given the war conditions, the consequent loss of handling was a fair trade off with the gain in power and speed achieved by the DB 605 installation. Many pilots in the field felt otherwise, claiming that the "G" series was a regressive step from the F series.

To house the DB 605A engine, no change was made in the upper contour of the cowling, however the oil cooler was deeper and of a slightly different shape, similiar to the "Z" option of the F. There were a number of differences in the panel lines forward of the cockpit especially around the windscreen where the lower oblique glass panel was deleted. The size of the supercharger intake was the same as the F-4 and the broad-bladed propeller of the "Z" became standard. However, without close examination the "Gustav" was in fact quite similar in appearance to its predecessor. A redesign of the fuel tank caused the fuel filler to be relocated from below the cockpit to the spine behind the cockpit. The wheel wells again reverted to the squared shape of the E and early F types in anticipation of covers that were never produced.

With the air war moving to ever higher altitudes, the need for a pressurized fighter dictated that the Gustav be produced with this provision. A *cold wall* type of pressurization was developed for the Bf 109G with the firewall, floor sidewalls and sloping armor plate behind the seat being sealed with rubber strips sealing the joints around the hinged canopy. The glazed panels of the greenhouse were layered with air sandwiched between them, a calcium chloride pellet maintained dryness. The pressurization resulted in a redesigned heavier canopy, sealed with rubber strips allowing a pressure differential of 4.4 LB/SQ FT. While pressurization was deleted on the majority of Gustavs, the provision was available on each machine by the addition of equipment. When pressurization was deleted, a small fresh air ventilation scoop was positioned just below the windscreen.

Production of the DB 605 powerplant was delayed, consequently the preproduction batch of twelve Bf 109G-0s were completed with DB 601E engines during fall and winter of 1941. The cowling and other external features of the G-0, however, were essentially the same as subsequent DB 605 equipped production machines. The DB 605A-1 was finally certified for production installation during early spring of 1942 with production of both the G-1 and G-2 commencing immediately. The pressurized G-1 and non-pressurized G-2 were run simultaneously on the assembly line, being essentially pressurized and un-

pressurized versions of the same variant, however, the Bf 109G-2 actually preceded the G-1s service introduction by several weeks.

Provision was made for installation of a GM 1 nitrous oxide power boost system, previously used on the 'Z' option powerboost system under the designation U-2. Weighing more than 400 LBS, the GM 1 nitrous oxide system, known as Goring's Mischung (Goring's mixture), had a tremendous affect on performance, not only allowing the G to operate above the rated altitude for the DB 605, but to literally leave a pursuing Spitfire V standing still.

A short time after service introduction of the G series, operational units began reporting mysterious fires shortly after take off, sometimes causing the loss of both aircraft and pilot. Testing eventually showed that during overheating the horseshoe shaped nose mounted oil tank seeped oil onto the hot engine, causing a flash fire. After ascertaining the problem, two small cooling scoops were introduced on each side of the nose, cooling the oil tank. General Kesselring and others have attributed the death of Hans-Joachim Marseilles to one of these oil fires, however, British Aviation Historian Jack Foreman has reported that a fracture in the glycol line was responsible for the fire that forced Marseille to fatally abandon his aircraft. Marseille was flying a Bf 109G-2 W. Mr. 14256.

Low oil pressure plagued the DB 605 engine throughout its operational career. Damiler-Benz maintained that the horseshoe oil tank was at fault while the Messerschmitt people claimed that the hydraulic supercharger trapped air bubbles in the oil. Eventually the DB people developed and installed a de-aerator but when no improvement was found the de-aerator was discarded. The oil pressure problem was never satisfactorily solved.

The G series was the true workhorse of the Luftwaffe's Day Fighter Units, with over 10,000 being produced in ten basic variants. Every day fighter unit and eight foreign countries used the 109G through the end of the war.

Bf 109 F-4

Bf 109 G-0

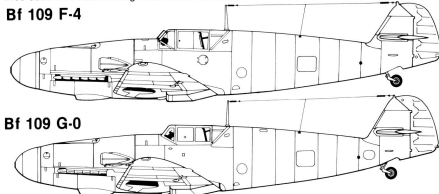

From the beginning the G series was designed to accept a variety of *Rustsatze* (field conversion sets). These bolt-on conversion kits allowed the Bf 109G to be readily converted from role to role in the field, although the *Rustsatze* were often installed at the factory. These conversion kits were numbered R-1 through R-7, with R-5 not being introduced.

R-1 ETC 900/IXb rack carrying a SC 250 bomb

R-2 ETC 50/VIId rack carrying 4 SC 50 bombs

R-3 300 liter droptank

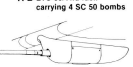

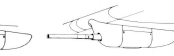

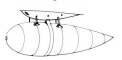

R-5 MK 108 30MM cannon under each wing

R-6 MG 151/20MM cannon under each wing

R-7 Direction Finding (DF) loop

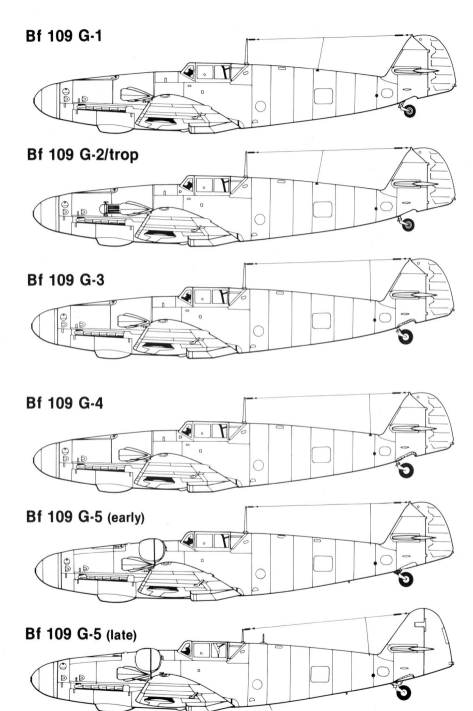

Bf 109 G-1

Bf 109 G-2/trop

Bf 109 G-3

Bf 109 G-4

Bf 109 G-5 (early)

Bf 109 G-5 (late)

Bf 109 G-6 (early)

Bf 109 G-6 (late)

Bf 109 G-6/AS (with tall tail)

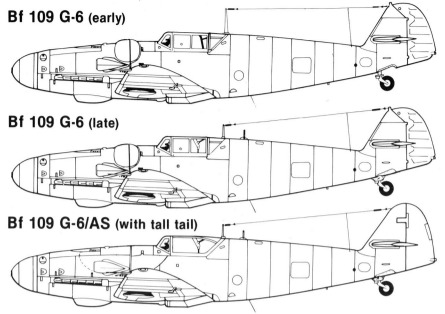

This Bf 109G-1 belonging to the Gruppen Adjutant of III/JG 52 on the southern sector of the Eastern front is having its engine oil filled. The tires are covered to prevent overheating in the hot sun. The heavy overspray behind the cockpit covers the factory assigned call letters, over which the chevron and number have been painted. JG 52 flew every model of the F and G over virtually every sector of the Eastern front.

Bf 109G-1
(Pressurized Fighter)

The pressurized Bf 109G-1 was run on the assembly line simultaneously with G-2, which was identical except for the G-2s lack of cabin pressurization.

The G-1 was first issued to those units facing Allied heavy bombers, primarily along the Channel Front and in North Africa. The first unit to receive the Bf 109G-1 was 1./JG 2 during the latter half of May 1942. During the summer, 11./JG 2, a special high altitude interceptor staffel, was formed and equipped with specially stripped down Bf 109G-1s carrying 300 litre drop tanks. Before long JG 26 formed a similar 11. Staffel

Front line pilots quickly found that the light armament of the G-1 was inadequate, as predicted, to seriously threaten the Allied heavy bomber formations which they were to face shortly. This lack of armament led to the G-1 being fitted with the R-6 option, a single MG 151 cannon mounted under each wing. While effective, this was another weight escalation and aerodynamic compromise.

Variants

Bf 109G-1/Trop Sand filters and desert survival equipment.
Rustsatze Fitted
R-1, R-2, R-3, R-6

During the spring and summer of 1942 both JG 2 *Richthofen* and JG 26 *Schlageter* formed special high altitude interceptor 11. Staffein based on GM 1 powerboosted Bf 108G-1/R-3s, a light wieght pressurized interceptor with the armor removed. 11./JG 2 is seen here carrying the "Bonzo" dog emblem of 1./JG 2 from which it has been formed.

Without changing the overall outside dimensions of the block, the DB 605 powerplant delivered considerably more power, which, when coupled with GM 1 had a phenomenal effect on performance. (Obert)

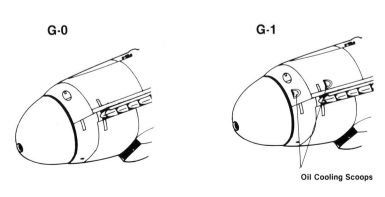

G-0   G-1

Oil Cooling Scoops

The Rustsatze 3, a 300 liter auxiliary fuel tank installation, had several differently shaped drop tanks available.

Droptanks

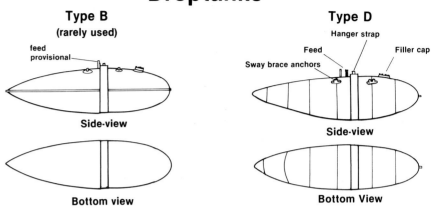

Type B
(rarely used)

feed
provisional

Side-view

Bottom view

Type D

Hanger strap

Feed

Filler cap

Sway brace anchors

Side-view

Bottom View

Type C

Bottom View

(Type E tank shown)

Side-view

Droptank

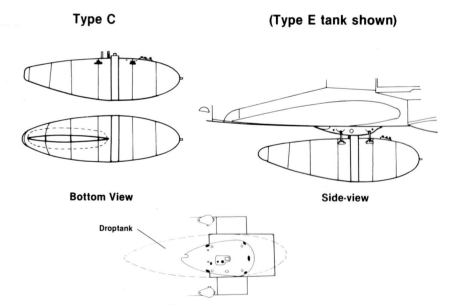

II/JG 52 flew the Bf 109G-1 in various locations on the central Russian front. The factory camouflage has been supplemented by a unique cowling camouflage design. This careful attempt at additional camouflage is ironic in view of the nice, tight line-up in completely open terrain. The third aircraft is purportedly that of Johannes Steinhoff, gruppen adjutant at the time.

Bf 109G-2 Fighter

Reaching operational status a few weeks before the G-1, was the G-2. Cabin pressurization was deleted with ventilation being provided by a pair of small fresh air scoops added just below the oblique windscreen panels—one scoop on each side. Radio equipment was still the same as the F-4, a FuG 7a and FuG 25 IFF. Standard armament was the engine mounted 20MM MG 151/20 cannon with 200 rounds and a pair of cowl-mounted 7.9 MG 17 machine guns with 500 rounds per gun. This could be supplemented by Rustsatze 6, a pair of MG 151/20 cannons in underwing gondolas. The G-2 quickly became the workhorse of the jadgruppen, appearing on all fronts as production would allow.

The first unit to receive the new machine was JG 2 *Richtofen* when *Stab* and I/JG 2 began to convert from the FW 190A during late April 1942. Walter Oesau, Kommodore of JG 2 again declined to fly the new Messerschmitt design, preferring to retain his FW 190.

Variants

Bf 109G-2/Trop
Rustsatze fitted: R-1, R-2, R-3, R-4, R-6

Pressurized G-1

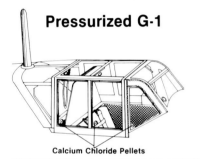

Calcium Chloride Pellets

Non-pressurized G-2

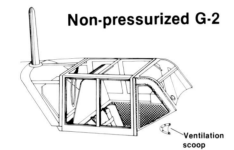

Ventilation scoop

Leading the Bf 109G-2 aircraft of JG 2 in his FW 190A-4, Walter Oesau begins another mission. JG 2, along with JG 26, held the "Channel Front" alone for many months in 1942. Eventually, pressure from USAAF and RAF raids forced the Luftwaffe to bring other units back to help defend France and Germany.

The Bf 109G-2 with its increased performance was well received on the Eastern Front, although pilots still complained of its lack of responsiveness. These machines belong to II/JG 52 during September 1942.

In response to the Soviet introduction of the Lavachkin La-5, an initial batch of 16 Bf 109G-2s were shipped to Finland during early 1943. HLeLv 34, to which these machines and pilots belong, destroyed 100 Russian aircraft for the loss of only seven of their own. (Obert)

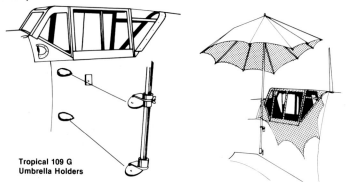

Tropical 109 G
Umbrella Holders

(Below Right) A Bf 109G-2 of a staffel leader from II/JG 53 reposes on a Tunisian airfield in the Spring of 1943. Its camouflage is Greys 74/75 over 76 supplemented by Green-Grey 02.

II/JG 53 "Pik As" flew the Bf 109G-2/R3 Trop from Sicily under II Fliegerkorps. The G/Trop carried a tubular dust filter of Italian design identical to the one carried on the F-series. In addition the G/Trop had two small blips on the fuselage under the port side of the canopy. These blips covered the attachment points for an umbrella which was used to shade the cockpit from the hot desert sun while the aircraft sat on the ground.

Bf 109G-3
(Pressurized Fighter)

By mid-1942, it had become obvious that the increasing weight of the G series required further refinements. To help ease the weight load and to improve handling on unpaved airfields, larger main wheels and tires as well as a larger tail wheel and tire were installed. The main wheels increased in size from 650mm x 150mm to 660mm x 160mm while the tail wheel increased from 290mm x 110mm to 350mm x 135mm. An external stiffener was added to the tail wheel opening, and a bulge was added to the top of the wings to accomodate the increased main wheel tire size. The tail wheel retraction unit was almost always locked down and fitted with a rubber dust cover.

The FuG 7a radio was replaced by FuG 16 necessitating a change in the antenna wire array.

Units known to have operated the G-3 include JG 3, JG 26, JG 27, JG 51, JG 52, JG 53 and JG 77. Several of these units saw service in Tunisia and Sicily, facing increasing numbers of Allied aircraft with their own numbers and skill levels dwindling.

Variants

Bf 109G-3/Trop
Rustsatze fitted: R-1, R-2, R-3, R-6.
Only the G-3/R-3 with the 300 litre drop tank saw extensive service on all fronts.

This Bf 109G-3/R-2 fighter/bomber in Rumanian service shows in clear silhouette the increased size of the new tail wheel introduced on the G-3. While the tail wheel was still retractable it was usually locked in the down position.

Landing Gear

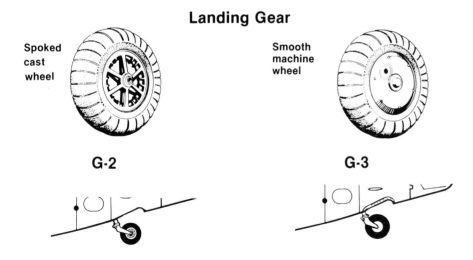

Spoked cast wheel

Smooth machine wheel

G-2

G-3

The oversized tires brought a degress of improved landing and ground handling characteristics which were especially welcomed on the Eastern Front, where fighters often operated from primitive forward airfields. The new stamped wheels that were introduced on the G-3 were considerably cheaper to produce than the spoked wheels, the spoked wheels continued to be used into 1944 however.

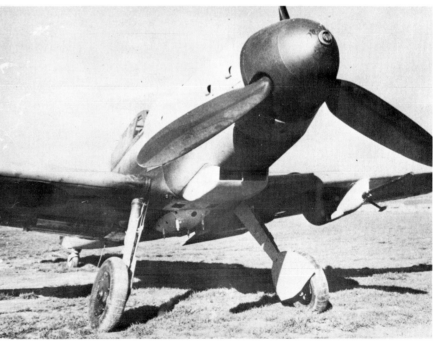

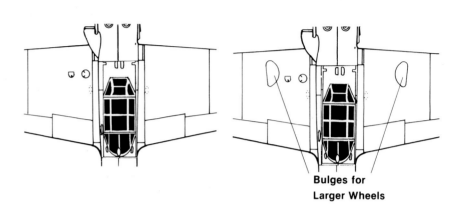

G-2

G-3

Bulges for
Larger Wheels

G-3 aircraft of III/JG 3 in southern Russia during 1943. The Gruppe Kommandeur's aircraft is in the foreground. The reposition of the radio aerial to accommodate the FuG 16z can be seen on this machine.

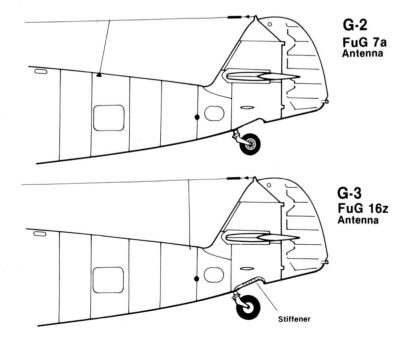

G-2
FuG 7a
Antenna

G-3
FuG 16z
Antenna

Stiffener

When local conditions required the use of a reconnaissance machine, ground crewmen rigged up this camera to shoot pictures through the windscreen. The worn rubber seal around the framing is part of the cabin pressurization equipment.

Bf 109G-4 (Non-pressurized Fighter)

Actually preceeding the G-3 on the production line, the Bf 109G-4 was identical to the G-3 except that it lacked pressurization. The G-4/R-3, the standard fighter, equipped with a 300 litre drop tank for extended range, was a large scale production model.

The G-4 also was one of the two reconnaissance models of the *Gustav* series. Under the designation G-4/R-2 the engine mounted MG 151/20 was deleted and a Rb 50/30 camera was installed in the fuselage behind the rear wing root. A 300 litre drop tank was normally carried. (F) 123 was known to have operated this version.

The G-4/R-6 was the first extensively produced Gustav to use the 20mm MG 151/20 cannon in under wing gondolas. Units known to have been issued aircraft carrying this armament are JG 3, JG 27 and JG 53, all of which operated against USAAF Bomber formations. The extra punch that the pair of underwing 20mm cannons provided was vital if fatal damage was to be done to these "heavies".

Variants

Bf 109G-4/Trop
Rustsatze
At least eight rustsatze (some numbers were used twice) were planned for the G-4 although few saw service.
R-1 Fighter Bomber limited production
R-2 Fighter Bomber limited production
R-3 Reconnaissance-not produced
R-4 Reconnaissance-not produced
R-7 Limited fitting of DF equipment
R-2 Reconnaissance Fighter
R-3 Fighter
R-6 Heavy Fighter

R-2 Camera Installation

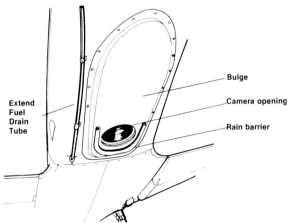

Extend Fuel Drain Tube

Bulge
Camera opening
Rain barrier

This Bf 109G-4/R-3/Trop of II/JG 27 also carries the R-6 consisting of a pair of 20mm MG 151/20 cannons in underwing gondolas. This was primarily in response to the introduction of the USAAF "heavies", the B-17 and B-24, which required considerable damage to bring down. This aircraft is being manhandled into a dispersal space in Tunisia during the Spring of 1943. Note the sealant over the engine mounted gun apperture in the spinner.

A Gruppe commander and his crew chief admire the newly painted rank chevrons on a 109G-4. The officer is wearing a "Herman Meyer" soft cap, a favorite with Luftwaffe troops in the Mediterranean. (Smithsonian)

These G-4 aircraft, believed to be from JG 4, are dispersed near a treeline on the Eastern Front. The nearest aircraft is a G-4/R-6 with the underwing 20mm cannon. JG 4 was transferred to Roumania during late Spring of 1943 and eventually fought the USAAF in the epic low-level raid of August 1 on the Ploesti oilfields. (Obert)

This G-4 of JG 26, carries the jagged edge camouflage pattern on its wings, characteristic of many G-4 aircraft. The four victory tallies on the rudder are over American aircraft. Note the semi-gloss finish of the paint which was characteristic of factory-fresh Luftwaffe aircraft.

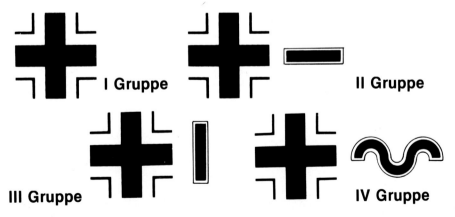

I Gruppe

II Gruppe

III Gruppe

IV Gruppe

Geshwader Kommodore Hannes Trautloft in front of his Bf 109-G in Russia during 1943. As is usual for JG 54 aircraft, this one has the two-tone Green camouflage and the Yellow fuselage band theater marking under the fuselage national insignia. (Obert)

Bf 109G-5
(Pressurized Fighter)

Since the introduction of the lightly armed Bf 109F, with its pair of cowl mounted MG 17s and single engine mounted MG 151, an armaments controversy had raged in the Luftwaffe's fighter arm. One faction claimed that a properly trained pilot should be able to use this light armament to bring down even the new USAAF "heavies" that were now pressing deeper into Germany. The other side argued that this was fine for the so called *Experten*, who for the most part had been trained under prewar or early war conditions, however, the fighter pilots entering front line service during 1942-43 were products of an abreviated training that provided only rudimentary gunnery training. The average pilot was simply not up to the same level of marksmanship or piloting as their predecessors. With the high speeds of 1942 allowing only a second or two on the target, and the advent of the USAAF "Heavies" with their tough construction, it was becoming obvious that more and heavier weapons were needed. The effectiveness of the Fw 190s hard hitting quartet of wing cannon and pair of cowl mounted machine guns helped to swing the argument in favor of the heavy armaments advocates. Unfortunately, the Focke Wulf's performance fell off at altitude.

The Bf 109G series suffered through "add-ons" such as the R-6 underwing gondolas to augment its fire power. The G-5 however replaced the cowl mounted 7.9MM MG 17 machine guns with a pair of 13MM MG 131 machine guns (which became the standard fuselage mounted armament for all subsequent Bf 109 models). The larger breech blocks and cocking mechanisms resulted in two bulges on the upper cowling just in front of the windscreen. The aircraft was immediately dubbed *buele* (bump) by its pilots, some of whom protested that this was another drag on a fighter that was already overweight and unresponsive. The gun troughs on the cowling were moved slightly to the rear and became a straight press rather than the insert found on the earlier G series.

The G-5 standardized the new cheaper machined wheels and larger tire sizes introduced on the G-3. In a quickie attempt to get more power for the much overloaded G-5, the GM-1 powerboost became virtually a standard fitting even though it was considered to be less effective than additional supercharging.

The G-5 was used extensively on all fronts, the most common versions being the G-5/R-3 fighter equipped with the 300 liter drop tank and the G-5/R-6 with the two MG 151/20 underwing cannons. Often the R-3 and R-6 were combined on the same aircraft, making it even heavier and more unresponsive. Such measures were necessary, however, to combat the increasingly large numbers of USAAF bombers over Western and Southern Europe.

Part way through the production run, further refinements were made to the G-5. A shorter antenna mast was introduced, and FuG 25a IFF radio equipment was installed resulting in a small whip antenna on the lower fuselage. A DF loop was added just behind the radio mast and a new type of pilot armor was fitted. Composed of thick armored glass in a metal frame, it was attached to the canopy just behind the pilot's head. The upper cowling was redesigned to accept a cheaper simplified punched out gun trough panels replacing the more expensive inserted troughs. A metal plate covering the tail wheel well was added and a rubber dust cover was fitted to the tail wheel oleo.

The Bf 109 had always swung on take-off and with hastily trained pilots, the higher powered, unresponsive G-5 was becoming a real handful at take-off. In an attempt to overcome this problem a new taller rudder with a straight hinge line was constructed of non-strategic wood and was fitted to some late production G-5 aircraft, but received no special designation.

In an attempt to get more basic power from the DB 605A engine, Daimler-Benz enlarged the supercharger. This resulted in the left engine bearer arm curving up over the supercharger. This was covered with longer more streamlined bulge to cover the supercharger and the MG 131 breech. This "refined" bulge was not quite symetrical, the starboard side bulge being slightly shorter. This aircraft was designated the Bf 109G-5/AS and was fitted with the tall tail. The G-5/AS was produced in very limited numbers and was known to have served with Aufkl.Gr.14 in the reconnaissance role as the Bf 109G-5/R-2/AS.

Variants

Bf 109G-5/Trop
Rustsatze   R-1, R-2, R-3, R-6

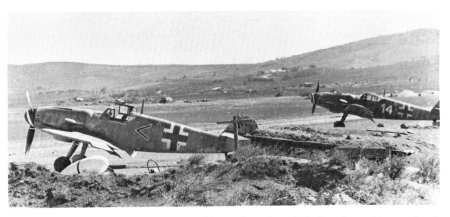

Two early production G-5 aircraft parked in semi-revetments in Russia next to a perimeter track. Both aircraft show extensive repainting of the fuselage sides indicating the aircraft have probably changed units. The presence of a drop tank in the foreground would indicate that the closest machine is an R-3, the aircraft at right however, lacks the under fuselage R-3 fittings.

Bf 109 G-1,2,3,4   **Bf 109 G-5 "Buele"**

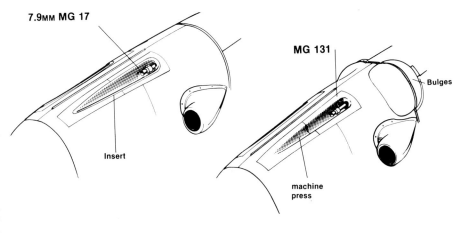

7.9MM MG 17

MG 131

Bulges

Insert

machine press

(Above and Below) Two views of one of the more famous 109G-5 aircraft, that of Hauptman Gerhard Barkhorn, Germany's second-ranked ace with 301 victories. *Christl* is white as is the small "5" which is a carry-over from an earlier aircraft flown by Barkhorn. This early production G-5 has the tailwheel fixed down with a rubber cover and the usual three-Grey camouflage.

A junkyard testament to the heavy losses suffered by the Geshwadern in Sicily in 1943. In the foreground is a 109G-5/Trop, believed to be of JG 51. To the right are more 109s and in the background, the wing of a FW 190. (IWM)

Tail Wheel

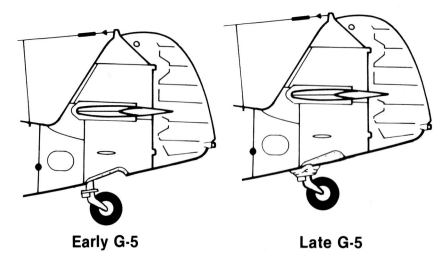

Early G-5　　　　**Late G-5**

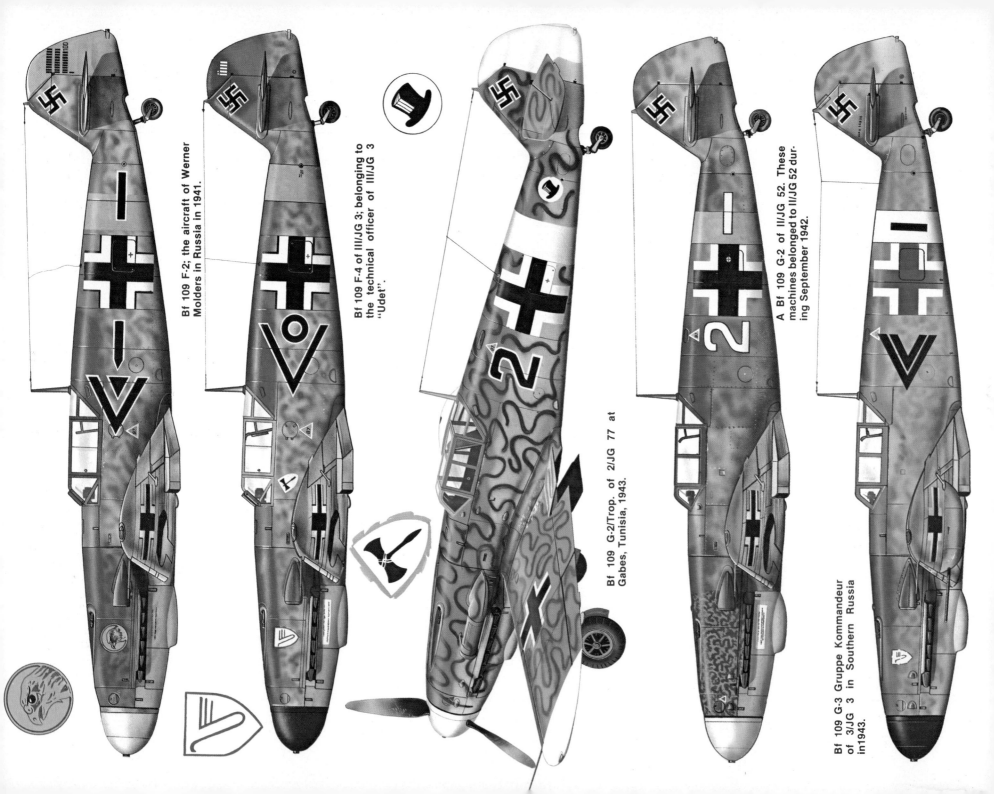

Bf 109 F-2; the aircraft of Werner Molders in Russia in 1941.

Bf 109 F-4 of III/JG 3; belonging to the technical officer of III/JG 3 "Udet".

Bf 109 G-2/Trop. of 2/JG 77 at Gabes, Tunisia, 1943.

A Bf 109 G-2 of II/JG 52. These machines belonged to II/JG 52 during September 1942.

Bf 109 G-3 Gruppe Kommandeur of 3/JG 3 in Southern Russia in 1943.

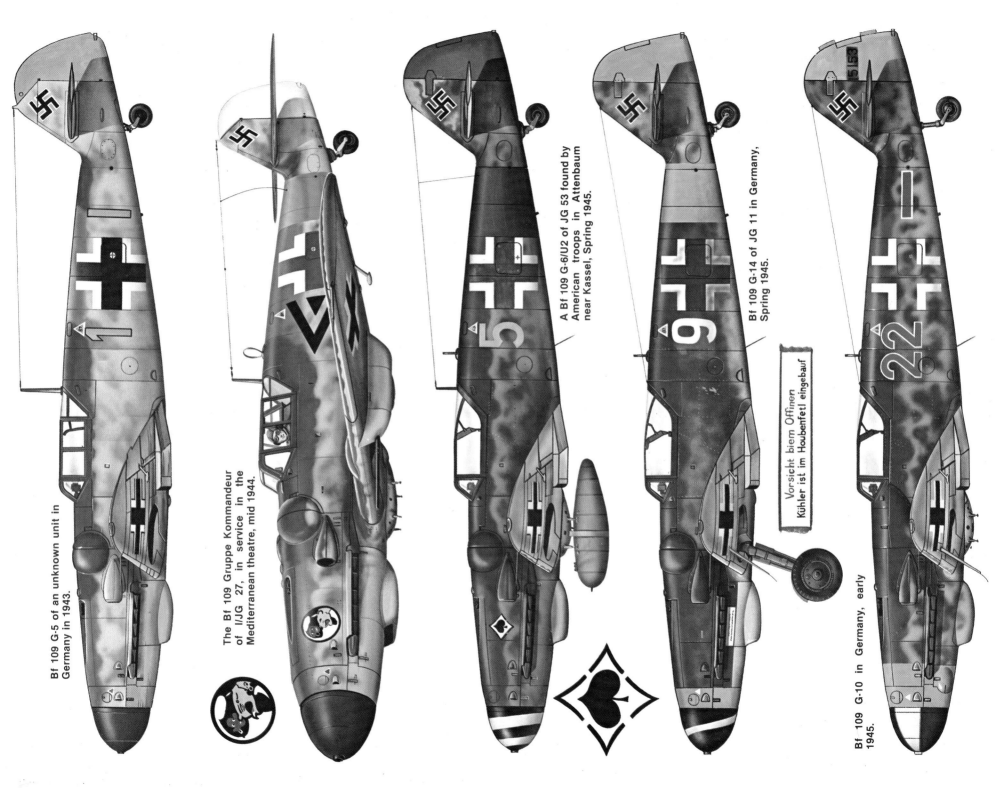

Bf 109 G-5 of an unknown unit in Germany in 1943.

The Bf 109 Gruppe Kommandeur of I/JG 27, in service in the Mediterranean theatre, mid 1944.

A Bf 109 G-6/U2 of JG 53 found by American troops in Attenbaum near Kassel, Spring 1945.

Bf 109 G-14 of JG 11 in Germany, Spring 1945.

Vorsicht biem Öffinen Kühler ist im Haubenfiefl eingebauf

Bf 109 G-10 in Germany, early 1945.

A mixture of early and late production G-5s from 9/JG 27 flying low over the Adriatic in late 1943. White 2 is a late production G-5, while 9 and 7 are early production G-5s although all three are equipped with FuG 25a IFF whip antennas. Also of interest is the variation in drop tanks.

Bf 109 G-5 (Late Production)

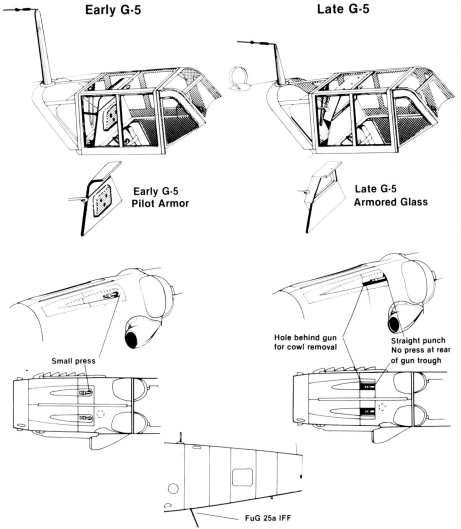

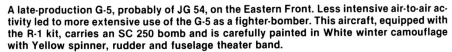

A late-production G-5, probably of JG 54, on the Eastern Front. Less intensive air-to-air activity led to more extensive use of the G-5 as a fighter-bomber. This aircraft, equipped with the R-1 kit, carries an SC 250 bomb and is carefully painted in White winter camouflage with Yellow spinner, rudder and fuselage theater band.

This G-5 belonging to a Gruppe commander sits in a crude revetment in Russia. As the Russian Air Force became more proficient, such precautions became a fact of life for the Luftwaffe in Russia. The aircraft is a late-production model with the short antenna mast, the DF loop, and the FuG 25a IFF antenna. Strangely, it has the early, rolled steel pilot armor. Just behind the IFF whip antenna can be seen the silhouette of the MW 50 boost tank drain tube.

G-5s of an unknown unit in Germany in 1943. The aircraft in the foreground, Yellow 1, is an early G-5 belonging to the staffel commander, while the machine in the background is a late G-5. In contrast to the casual dispersement of these aircraft, something in the background is very heavily camouflaged with netting.

A late Bf 109G-5/R-3 with the tall wooden tail taxies out for another mission. The aircraft, belonging to a staffel commander, is probably from JG 3, one of the first units pulled back for defense of the homeland. Note the Red trim tab contrasting on the White rudder. The camouflage is the usual Grays, 74/75 over 76, but with very strong spotting of 74, 75 and Green/Grey 02.

G-5 Tail Development

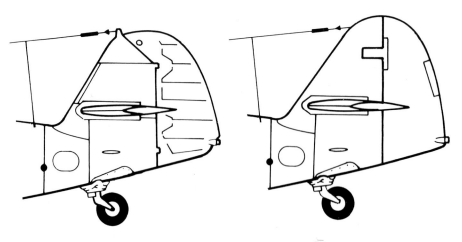

Standard Tail   **Tall Wooden Tail**

Bf 109G-6 Fighter

Bf 109 G-6 Late production

Like the Bf 109G-1 and G-2 the Bf 109G-5 and G-6 were produced in parallel and were essentially pressurized and nonpressurized versions of the same variant. The non-pressurized Bf 109G-6 was much more numerous than the G-5, more widely used and was also much longer-lived, being introduced in early 1943 and still in first line service in 1945. Initially the only external difference between the G-6 and the G-5 was the small fresh air intake scoop found on either side of the windscreen of the nonpressurized G-6. All modifications made to the G-5 air frame were also made to the G-6, however, because of its much longer production life the G-6 evolved through additional changes after production of the pressurized G-5 was terminated.

The stepped-up Allied bomber offensive against Germany and occupied Europe, forced the Luftwaffe to use the now elderly Bf 109G series in a variety roles to try to counter the overwhelming numbers of Allied planes. The Fw 190, while a more ideal bomber intercepter because of its heavy armament, did not have the altitude performance necessary, nor the numbers to effectively stem the tide. The Bf 109G-6 was jury-rigged into a number of roles for which it was unsuited and its performance suffered further. When combined with less capable pilots, this resulted in devastation to the Bf 109G-6 units, who were hunted by packs of P-51 Mustangs and P-47 Thunderbolts during 1944. The most widely produced versions of the G-6 were the R-3 fighter (300 liter drop tank), the R-6 fighter (MG 151/20 underwing guns) and the R-2 reconnaissance fighter (Rb 50/30 camera installation). Considerable experimentation took place with the 21cm BR 21 underwing air-to-air rockets, but they proved unsuitable and were seldom used operationally except by a few test groups.

Early production G-6 aircraft, like its pressurized counterpart, had a tall radio mast, however, the majority of G-6 aircraft built were in the late configuration equipped with the short radio mast, FuG 25A IFF and whip antenna, and the R-7 radio DF loop. The tall wooden tail was also used extensively by the G-6. Introduced on a few G-5 aircraft, the *erla haube* canopy was widely used on very late production G-6 machines. Sometimes incorrectly called the "Galland hood", this canopy replaced the main canopy and rear section with a single clear canopy with two thin frames on either side of the top. Because of its excellent visibility the *erla haube* proved to be very popular, although there were complaints that it was difficult to open during an emergency.

Cooling problems had always plagued the Bf 109G series and with the advent of the Bf 109G-6/Trop a fix was made on two areas of cooling (these were, of course, also found on a few G-5/Trop aircraft). First, a small scoop was added to the Mg 131 bulge on the right side of the cowling to provide additional cooling to the generator. Also on the right side, just in front of the scoop was added a small bulged cover to accomodate a larger oil pump.

Like the G-5, some G-6 aircraft were fitted with the DB 605AS engine with increased supercharging resulting in the asymetrical "refined" cowling bulges. Bf 109G-6AS aircraft were known to have served with JG 1, JG 11, JG 27, JG 53.

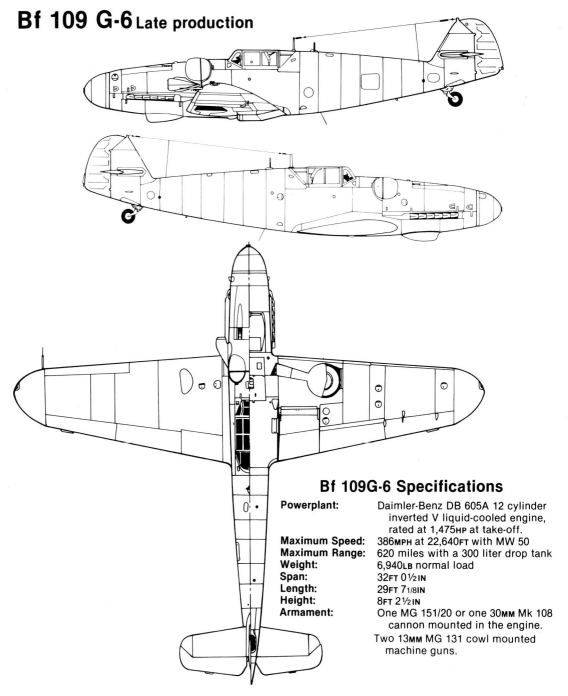

Bf 109G-6 Specifications

Powerplant: Daimler-Benz DB 605A 12 cylinder inverted V liquid-cooled engine, rated at 1,475hp at take-off.

Maximum Speed: 386mph at 22,640ft with MW 50

Maximum Range: 620 miles with a 300 liter drop tank

Weight: 6,940lb normal load

Span: 32ft 0½in

Length: 29ft 7 1/8in

Height: 8ft 2½in

Armament: One MG 151/20 or one 30mm Mk 108 cannon mounted in the engine.

Two 13mm MG 131 cowl mounted machine guns.

These early production G-6 aircraft await unit assignment on a German airfield. Most frequently, second-level centers received these aircraft and equipped them with the various Rüstsätze.

Bf 109 G-6   Bf 109 G-6/Trop

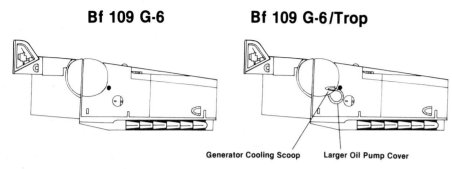

Generator Cooling Scoop   Larger Oil Pump Cover

(Below Right) Not only an *Experten* but an expert with the 109G, is Gerhard Barkhorn, the 2nd ranked Ace of all-time, seen here receiving congratulations from his Gruppe after his 250th victory. Barkhorn's Bf 109G-6, like his G-5, carried the name *Christl* and his Kommodore Chevrons carried the numeral 5 from his original aircraft. (Hans Rossbach)

The summer of 1943 found several German units defending Sicily against heavy Allied air combat, among them, these early production G-6/R-3/R-6 aircraft of II/JG 53 at Gerbini. Aside from missions, which found them always outnumbered, the heat of Sicily was a factor as the tarps over the wheels and cockpits of these aircraft indicate. II/JG 53 was so decimated in the battles over Sicily, that it was withdrawn to Austria to reform.

This late production G-6 of JG 54 illustrates typical conditions of the Eastern Front in 1943/44: open dispersal and snow-covered grass airfields. This aircraft has large areas of its original Grey camouflage left uncovered by the temporary White paint. Typical for JG 54, the lower rudder is Yellow and the Yellow Eastern Front color band is behind the fuselage cross. The bulging plate covering the larger oil pump can be seen just in front and below the gun bulges.

(Below Left) One Gruppe (about 40 aircraft) of JG 53, along with elements of JG 4, JG 51, and Italian R.S.I. units, were left to defend northern Italy against the 12TH and 15TH U.S.A.A.F.s and the R.A.F.'s Desert Air Force in 1944. With the Alps as a backdrop, the ground crew of *Gruppen Kommandeur* Jurgen Harder of I/JG 53 work on the underwing cannon of Harder's G-6/R-6 as Harder looks on. The aircraft is also fitted with the R-3 drop tank. Behind the drop tank is very clearly silhouetted the FuG 25a IFF whip antenna.

As the 15TH AAF began to make its presence felt in Austria and Hungary, Hungarian Air Force units were recalled from the Eastern Front to defend the homeland. USAAF reports frequently led one to believe that Germans were doing the fighting, but most bomber missions were opposed by Hungarian, German and Italian R.S.I. units. This G-6 is camouflaged in the typical German Greys with a Yellow rudder, Black codes, White band, and the national insignia Grey with Black edging. The machine in the foreground is a late production G-6 while the aircraft in the background is an early production G-6 with the tall antenna and open tail wheel well. A Heinkel He 111Z "Zwilling" can be seen in the background.

I/JG 27, after being involved in the heavy battles over Sicily and Italy, was returned to reform as part of Luftflotte Reich, defending against the USAAF. This G-6/R-3/R-6, belonging to the *Gruppen Kommandeur,* exhibits the camouflage and markings typical of mid-1944. The White rudder is a carry-over of the unit's Mediterranean service. A new addition is the Green fuselage band which indicates service in direct defense of the Reich.

As fuel supplies became the bete noir of the Luftwaffe, all measures to conserve fuel were taken, including pushing aircraft instead of taxiing, as the ground crew of this II/JG 2 G-6/R-6 is doing. Note that this late model G-6 has the small scoop and bulge near the hand crank. This aircraft also has the wing root and the fuselage near the wing root painted Black.

The 109G-6/R-3 with the tall tail came into service in late 1943. Many were fitted with the clear *erla haube* canopy, as is this aircraft of I/JG 11.

Bf 109 G-6 (Late) With Tall Tail

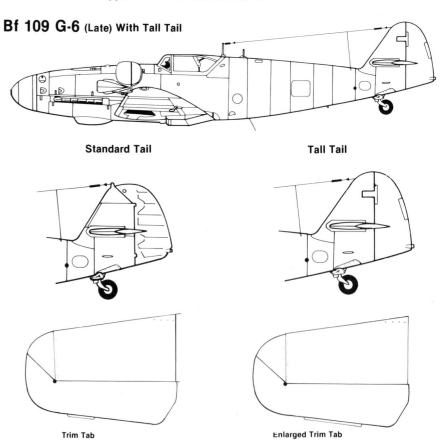

Standard Tail   **Tall Tail**

Trim Tab   Enlarged Trim Tab

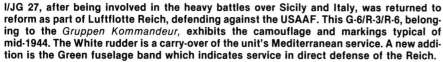

Bf 109G-8
Reconnaissance Fighter

The Bf 109G-8 was not really a new variant of the G series, it was a conversion of the G-6 airframe with the addition of fuselage mounted cameras. A short range, tactical reconnaissance aircraft whose timely introduction over the battlefields of 1944 served to provided sorely needed information on the movement of Allied Forces sweeping across Western Europe. The G-8 differed from earlier Bf 109 reconnaissance types by having two fuselage camera positions (between the 5th and 6th fuselage frames) slightly oblique, staggered and each covered with a square shaped sliding metal panel. A third camera was located in the leading edge of the left wing, which was sighted via the gunsight and could be used for single frame oblique photos.

The two produced types were the R-2 and the R-5 which differed primarily in the types of cameras installed, although the R-5 frequently deleted the engine mounted MG 151/20 cannon. The R-2 also had the MW 50 boost and a 300 liter drop tank. Both aircraft retained the fuselage mounted MG 131 machine guns. Some G-8 aircraft were seen with the deeper oil cooler and broad bladed propeller used by later production G types. It is not known, however, if these were factory fitted items or field modifications by units acting on their own. Few of the late production Bf 109G-8s were fitted with the clear *erla haube* canopy, although almost all aircraft were fitted with the R-7 DF loop.

The G-8 is known to have served with the short range reconnaissance units *NAG* 5, *NAG* 8, *NAG* 15, the reconnaissance Gruppe Aufkl.Gr.14 and with the Finnish Air Force.

Bf 109 G-8 Camera Arrangement

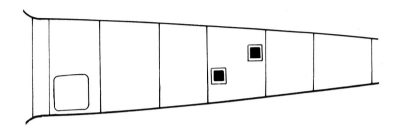

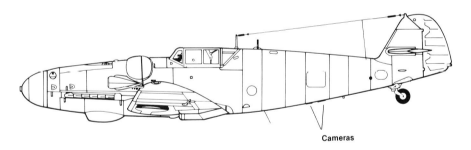

Cameras

A Bf 109G-8 which crashed on the Anzio Front during early 1944. Luftwaffe units in Italy were reduced to near impotence after the fall of 1943. JG 27, parts of JG 51, 53 and 77 were transferred to Austria and Germany, to *Luftflotte Reich,* to defend against USAAF raids. This left elements of JG 4, 51 and 53 to defend against overwhelming odds. The reconnaissance units in Italy often could complete their missions only under fortuitous circumstances. This aircraft, Yellow 6 is camouflaged with Greys 74 and 75 over 76. The very unusual sawtooth edge, between the upperwing surface colors, is typical of many aircraft assigned to recon units. The fuselage sides are heavily spotted with the two Greys and Grey Green 02. The White fuselage band is, of course, typical for all Luftwaffe aircraft assigned to the Mediterranean Theater. (IWM)

Bf 109G-12 Trainer

Before the war, and during the early war years, the Luftwaffe had provided themselves with excellent but leisurely trained pilots, little thought had been given to dual-place trainer versions of operational aircraft like the Bf 109. However with the push for a shorter and shorter training syllabus during 1942/43, it was felt that a dual-place version of the Bf 109G would help considerably. The aircraft, designated Bf 109G-12 was not as successful as hoped. Not a purpose-built airframe, but converted from randomly selected G-2, G-4 and G-6 airframes (even a few DB 605AS versions were built). Of the 900 G-12 aircraft projected, less than 100 were completed.

The G-12 was arranged so that the student sat in the front seat, he got the exact conditions that the student would get if he were flying alone. He was sitting in the same position in comparison to the wing—it was just like sitting in a G-6 or G-14.

When taking off the pilot can see nothing. We had to solo at least twelve times in the G-12—I tell you I was scared shitless—I sweat just to think about it.

Flieger Officier Herman Leypoldt

G-12 rebuilt from G-6 Air Frame

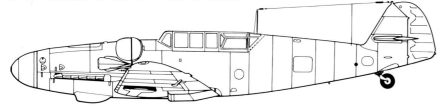

G-12 Cockpit

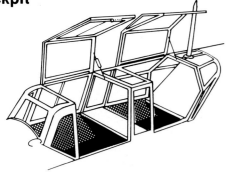

A G-12, converted from a G-6 airframe, rests on a paddock at a permanent German airbase. The conversion appears to be brand-new as the canopy frames are unpainted and the radio call codes have been cut through during the conversion. This was originally a purpose-built G-6/Trop as the umbrella holders indicate.

A G-12, Yellow 27, in 1944 was originally a G-2 airframe. These aircraft were not successful and their numbers gradually lessened as the war went on until only a few were left at the war's end.

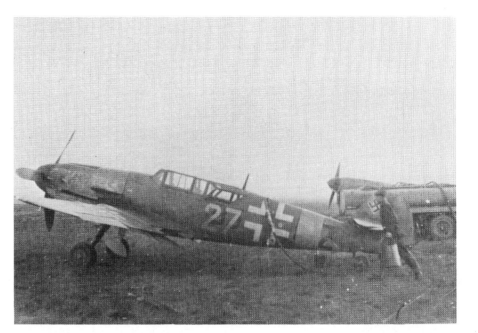

Bf 109G-14 Fighter

The 109G-5 was the last production version to have cockpit pressurization. The G-7, G-9, and G-11 numbers were reserved for pressurized types, but were never produced.

Although not numerically next, the 109G-14 was produced after the G-6 when the G-10 was delayed pending production of the DB 605D engine.

Meanwhile, the war went on. More fighters were needed, but poor planning for new types and bottlenecks in production of existing fighters inhibited maximum production. In an attempt to bring some direction and coherance to fighter production, the *Jager Stab,* or Fighter Staff, a special committee, was formed to ruthlessly deal with all bottlenecks and problems in the production of the 109 or any other fighter. The G-14 was the result of this committee's first attempt to rationalize the many options and variants of the 109G that were inhibiting maximum production of the aircraft. After a few early production aircraft that appeared similar to the G-6, the G-14 standardized on the tall wooden tail (with two external trim tabs and one inset), the *erla haube* canopy and the DB 605A engine. Almost all aircraft had the standard wheels and tires but a few late-production aircraft had the wider main wheels and tires. The small generator cooling scoop and bulge for the larger oil pump that had appeared on the tropical version of the G-5 and G-6 were standardized on the G-14.

A few reconnaissance G-14 aircraft were produced under the designation G-14/R-2, however, the vast majority of G-14 aircraft were produced with the drop tank rack under the designation G-14/R-3. Like the G-5 and G-6, some G-14 aircraft received the DB 605AS engine with its increased performance and was much more widely used than the earlier types. Its external appearance differed in that it used a new, increased capacity nose oil cooler that resulted in a deep-section cowl covering. The G-14AS is known to have served with JG 4, JG 6 and JG 27.

Although inferior in performance to other late G and K aircraft, the G-14 was produced in significant numbers and was widely used until the end of the war. Units known to have operated the G-14 were JG 1, JG 3, JG 7, JG 11, JG 27, JG 53 and JG 300.

The summer of 1944, found the Luftwaffe in the West, harassed from every quarter. This was especially true in Normandy and Eastern France where droves of Allied aircraft awaited the appearance of any German fighter in the air or on the ground. This G-14 probably of JG 3, is heavily camouflaged in its revetment while undergoing maintenance. Missions were infrequent due to dwindling fuel allotments.

Erla Haube Canopy

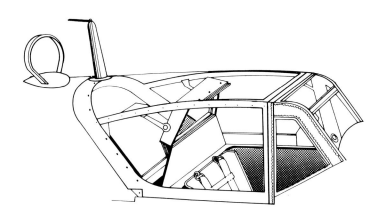

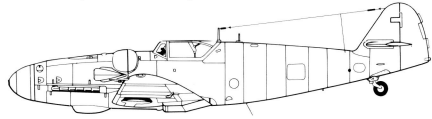

Bf 109 G-14

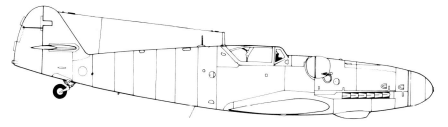

This G-14 is reputed to be that of Lt. "Ossie" Romm of 4/JG 3 photographed in the fall of 1944. It has a very unusual camouflage pattern. The basic colors are Green 82 and Green 83 with the fuselage sides very heavily spotted with the same two colors. Why the fuselage cross and the swastika is overpainted is unknown.

Bf 109 G-14

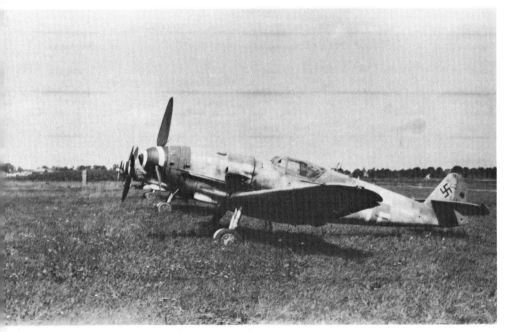

As the Luftwaffe retreated to its German and Dutch bases during the Fall of 1944, these more permanent bases were vulnerable to Allied air attack. This base is undergoing repair as a G-14 taxis by on the perimeter track. This aircraft, possibly of JG 3, indicates the nature of its short-range missions by the lack of a drop tank.

Bf 109 G-14AS

The changes incorporated into the 109G-14 when it was powered by the DB 605AS engine, the refined cowling bulges over the 13mm MG 131 guns and the reshaped engine bearer, the deeper oil cooler under the nose.

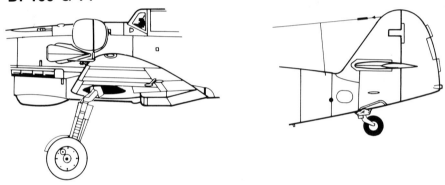

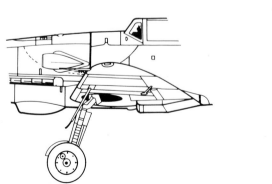

A G-14 of an unknown second gruppe on a German airfield during the sumer of 1945. G-14s were produced and served until the end of the war. This particular aircraft has a Yellow nose band and rudder. The aircraft appears to have a faded camouflage of Greys 76, 74, and 75. (Steve Cook Collection)

A typical scene toward the end of the war at many German airbases: This G-14 and a G-6 have been totally destroyed after an air raid. The base was subsequently captured by the U.S. 30th division, "Old Hickory", from North Carolina. (USAF)

Reichsverteidigund

Defense of the Reich

As the USAAF's bombing campaign got into high gear during 1944, the Luftwaffe was forced to transfer more and more fighter units back to Germany. Among these were JG 27, JG 51, JG 53 and JG 77. JG 2 and JG 26 were already in the low countries and France, and JG 1 and JG 11 were in Germany and Denmark. All these units were flying the Bf 109G. In addition there also were a miscellany of specialized units, and as the Germans regained control of the night skies, the *Wilde Sau* Geschwadern JG 300 and JG 301 were posted to the day fighters, specializing in bad weather interception. With this influx of fighter planes and the advent of American aircraft that were now ranging the length and breadth of Germany, the Luftwaffe recognized that some sort of fighter recognition feature was required to help the Luftwaffe fighters quickly recognize each other during the heat of battle.

Although no written record survives, as early as 1943, the Germans apparently attempted some sort of recognition for fighters (beyond the standard theater markings), many of them appeared with most or all of their vertical tail surfaces painted white. Units known to have used these white tail markings were JG 1, JG 11, JG 26, JG 27 (while in Southern Europe), and JG 52 (while still in Southeast Europe). These white markings were apparently unsatisfactory since they had largely disappeared by early 1944.

During the summer of 1944, just after D-Day, distinctive markings began to appear again. The first units to use them appear to be JG 1, JG 3 and JG 27. These markings took the form of color bands around the rear fuselage. Again there is no surviving record of an order specifying these bands, but appearing as they did almost simultaneously, there must have been some sort of official action or sanction. Known defense of the Reich colors on Bf 109 aircraft are as follows:

JG	1	Red	JG 51	Green/White/Green
JG	3	White	JG 52	Red/White
JG	4	Black/White/Black	JG 53	Black
JG	5	Black/Yellow	JG 77	White/Green
JG	11	Yellow	JG 300	Blue/White/Blue

The size of the band varied, JG 1 and JG 27 being wide and JG 3 being quite narrow. As the Summer and Fall of 1944 wore on, more units began adopting these colorful markings. Finally in January, 1945, the Luftwaffe made the application of the "Defense of the Reich" fuselage bands official by issuing an order that all units use them. Not all did, but remarkably, with all the other problems at the time, most units did use the bands, among them all Bf 109 units in action (not all aircraft in the unit however).

Towards the end of the war, during the Spring of 1945, a further change took place. Again no official order has survived, but several units began applying color bands around the cowling just behind the spinner. Photographically there has been no consistancy found in the placement of these nose bands, they seem to have varied from aircraft to aircraft. The nose band did not replace the fuselage bands although they did on some aircraft. The colors used were Red, Yellow, Green, and White. Several Bf 109G and K-4 were seen to sport these bands including aircraft of JG 11, JG 27, JG 53 and JG 301.

In late Spring, just before the final collapse of the Reich, some units began over painting the nose, or the fuselage bands, or both, with dark greens. There has been some thought that these were temporary tactical colors not directly related to an official defense band.

Defense of The Reich

1943

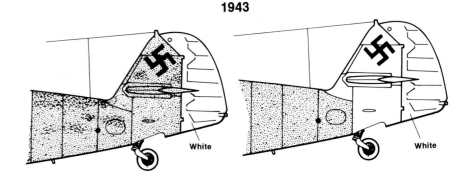

White

White

1944/45

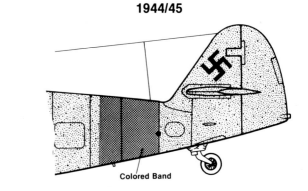

Colored Band

Last Months

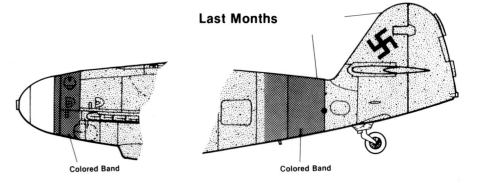

Colored Band

Colored Band

A Bf 109G-6 flown by Alfred Grislawski, a Knight's Cross holder. At this time he was assigned to Jagdgruppe 50, a special unit. The photo was taken in September, 1943 when Grislawski had 112 of his eventual 133 victories. The solid White vertical fin and rudder is clearly evident in the photo. Note also the very soft division line between the uppersurface colors on the tail plane and wing.

(Above Right) A late G-6, Yellow 8 of I/JG 27 poses on an airfield in the summer of 1944. The unit had White rudders and the Green defense band on the rear fuselage is clearly evident. This appeared about the same time as the Red band of JG 1 and the White band of JG 3.

A quiet scene, but the heavy camouflage paint and netting shows that action is anticipated at this German airfield. This Bf 109G-14, White 9, of JG 11 is heavily camouflaged with colors 81 and 82 on its fuselage sides. The aircraft clearly illustrates the Yellow Defense band worn by aircraft of this unit. This aircraft is also wearing a Yellow rudder and a Yellow band around the forward cowling, behind the propeller. (IWM)

Bf 109G-10

By 1944, the Luftwaffe was caught in a vicious cycle. The increased ferocity of the airwar meant more losses as well as a basic need for more aircraft and pilots. More losses meant more pilots needed. This, in turn, meant more hastily-trained pilots who could not handle their aircraft and, consequently, heavier pilot losses. A contributor to this endless cycle was the Bf 109G, which by now was overweight and slow. In the hands of the legendary "experten" it was still capable of besting its opponents, but the average Luftwaffe pilot was simply incapable of accomplishing this.

In an attempt to increase the speed of the 109G, the DB 605D engine was developed. Similiar to the DB 605AS, the DB 605D's supercharger was increased in size, and again, the compression ratio was increased as well as the displacement. The MW 50 boost was retained, and as a result, the G-10 was the fastest of the entire G series.

Standard equipment for the G-10 was the FuG 25a IFF, a DF loop, the tall wooden tail, the *erla haube* canopy, and the FuG 16ZY with the Moranne mast under the left wing. The DB 605D, of course, employed the refined cowling, enlarged supercharger intake, deeper oil cooler, and wider propeller blades all of which appeared on the G-14AS. One further difference in the appearance of the G-10 was the addition of two bulges on either side of the lower cowling resulting from enlarged oil sumps and camshaft covers.

Some production models of the G-10 received wings with the normal size wheel well bulges and tires of the G-6/14 type. These aircraft also had the long shaft, fixed tailwheel and no external trim tabs on the rudder. The extended length tailwheel was another attempt to help the pilot see over the cowl and give a better angle of attack during take-off. Other G-10 aircraft received the larger, wider main wheels with the wings having large uppersurface rectangular wheel well bulges. These aircraft had two external, fixed rudder trim tabs and the normal, short fixed tailwheels. The manuals stated that these G-10s were to be fitted with the extended length tailwheels at field modification centers and many were.

The G-10 was issued to units in early fall, 1944, coinciding with a slight resurgence of the Luftwaffe day fighter units. More aircraft were produced in November, 1944 than at any time during the war, many of them being Bf 109s. However, a fuel shortage and poorly trained pilots combined to prevent any dramatic reversal of fortune. Units known to have operated the G-10 are JG 1, JG 3, JG 4, JG 5, JG 6, JG 11, JG 27, JG 52, JG 53, JG 300, some Hungarian, Croatian and Italian RSI units.

White 4 of an unknown unit sits on Kassel airfield in February, 1945. This G-10, which has the normal main wheels and long tailwheel, clearly illustrates a late-war 109 camouflage pattern using colors 76/81/82. The Werk No. 6316, is in an unusual location on the fuselage instead of the normal late-war position on the fin and rudder.

G-10 Tail Development

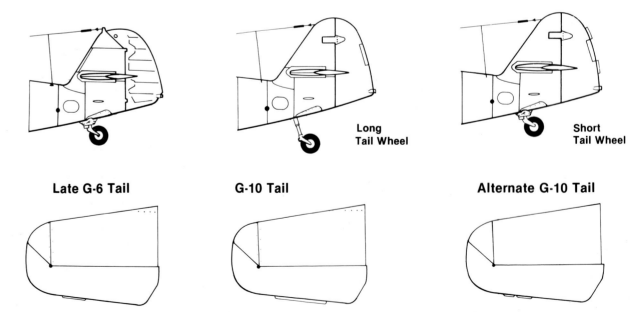

Long Tail Wheel

Short Tail Wheel

Late G-6 Tail   G-10 Tail   Alternate G-10 Tail

(Above) At the end of the war, Luftwaffe aircraft were abandoned everywhere. This G-10, Yellow 7, carries the Blue-White-Blue band of JG 300. It appears that a color was applied around the cowling behind the spinner but was overpainted with Black-Green 70. This aircraft has the long tail wheel and enlarged main wheels. (Frantisek Sazel)

(Below) Another G-10 at the end of the war, this time in Northern Italy. This aircraft, Black 4, of the Croation Air Force shows several interesting markings. The normal Yellow fuselage band has been painted over, and Yellow painted around the cowl behind the spinner. This may indicate an attempt to comply with some order as discussed in the text. The rudder is Yellow and the Ustachi emblem with a Red and White shield is seen on the tail. The uppersurface colors are 81/82 Greens. This G-10 has the normal main wheels and wing bulges, the long-stroke fixed tailwheel, and no external rudder trim tabs. (USAF)

This G-10 illustrates the prime identity characteristics of the variant: The deep nose oil cooler, the refined cowl bumps covering the MG 131 guns and the larger supercharger intake. This aircraft is unusual in that it has the short fixed tailwheel and the normal wheels and wing bulges. Note the oil on the drop tank coming from a leak in the oil cooler, characteristic of the DB 605 engine.

Engine Development

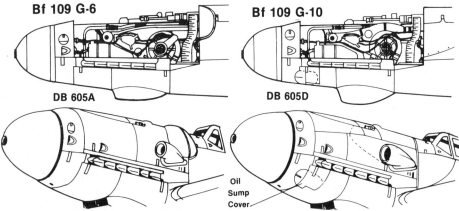

Bf 109 G-6

DB 605A

Bf 109 G-10

DB 605D

Oil Sump Cover

A Gustav pilot of II/JG 27 in Prossnitz, Czechoslovakia in the spring of 1945. The Green tailband of JG 27 is clearly visable. The rudder appears to have been repainted a light color, perhaps Yellow. This G-10 has the extended tailwheel leg. (Steve Cook Collection)

In spite of the wider tires, longer tailwheels and other improvements, the narrow track landing gear remained an inherent weakness of the Bf 109 and this G-10, "Red 22", illustrates in this landing accident. This aircraft (Werk No. 1513) has the wide main wheels and rectangular bumps. The camouflage is 76/81/82 with a Yellow rudder and noseband. Note the sheen of the camouflage paint, a characteristic of German paints when fresh. This aircraft is equipped with the R-3 drop tank rack.

White 1, a G-10 with the wide main wheels, at Munich airfield in June, 1945. Note the large size of the upper wing crosses which are merely White outlines. The large upper wing wheel well bulges and camouflage pattern are clearly visable. (Steve Cook Collection)

A view of Black 2, a staff aircraft. This G-10 has the wider main wheels and the enlarged upper wing wheel well blisters are clearly evident. These photographs, taken in the Summer of 1945, also illustrate that the starboard side of the rudder is Black. This might indicate that the unit was JG 53 which flew G-10s until the end of the war. The port side of the rudder was a solid color, perhaps Yellow. The camouflage appears to be 76/81/82. The aircraft clearly illustrates the change in the antenna lead-in location: it did not use the mast, but went directly into the fuselage behind the canopy. (Steve Cook Collection)

G-10 Development

Early	Late

Long Tail Wheel

Short Tail Wheel

G-10 was often field modified to long tail wheel configuration

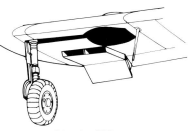 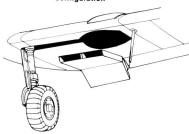

Standard Tires

Wide Tires

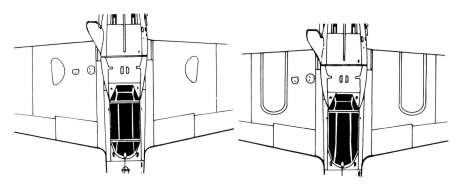

Standard Tire Bumps   **Wide Tire Bumps**

Red 19, a Bf 109-G-10 of 6/JG 77 in sad conditioning at Muhlheim am Ruhr in late fall of 1944. This aircraft belonged to UFFz. Karl Muller and was hit by a Bf 110 landing at night. At this stage of the war, day and night fighter units often shared airfields in order to utilize flak units which were set up in special zones to protect against marauding Allied fighters. The aircraft appears to have a temporary camouflage net, perhaps to help hide the aircraft until it can be moved to cover. (James Crow)

Antenna Mast Lead in

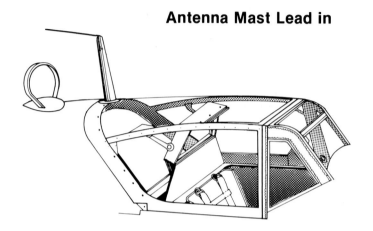

Alternate Antenna Lead in

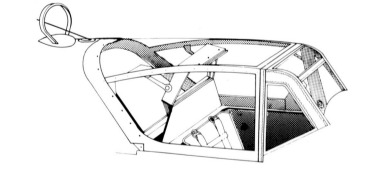

A G-10, believed to be of JG 51, on VE-Day at Munchen airfield. The pilot posed for the photo before getting out and surrendering. Note the name *Rosemarie* and the White 11 that have been painted over a previous number. The antenna lead-in can be seen just ahead of the DF loop, going directly into the fuselage. (Steve Cook Collection)

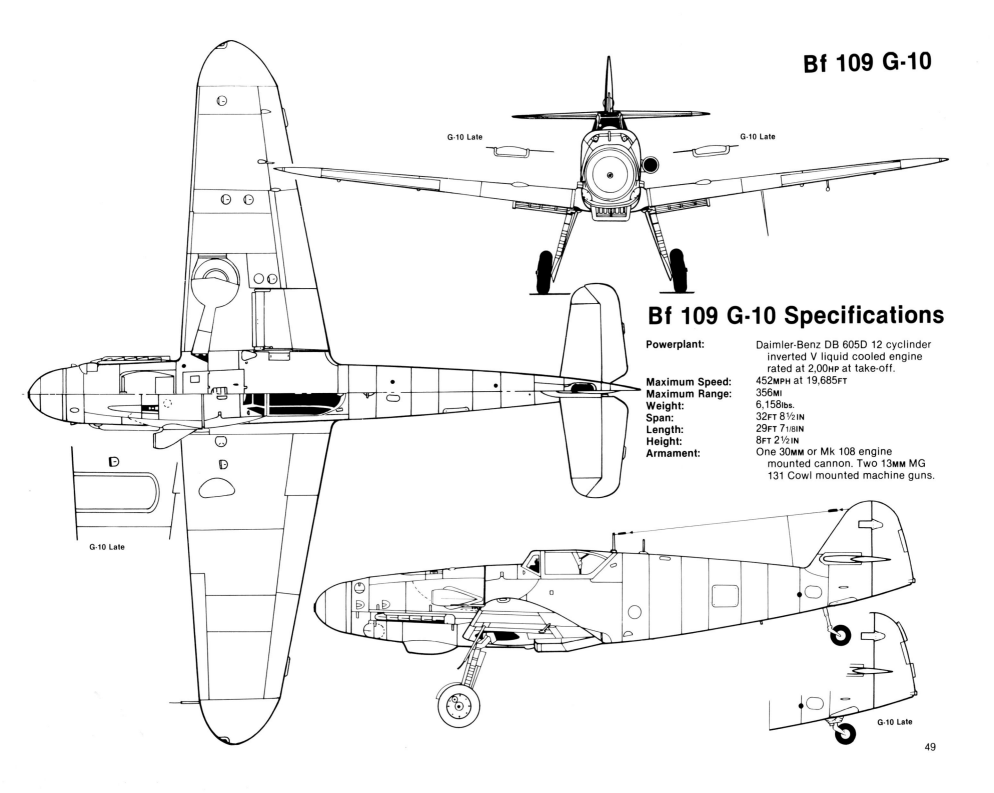

Bf 109 G-10

G-10 Late

G-10 Late

G-10 Late

G-10 Late

Bf 109 G-10 Specifications

Powerplant:	Daimler-Benz DB 605D 12 cyclinder inverted V liquid cooled engine rated at 2,00HP at take-off.
Maximum Speed:	452MPH at 19,685FT
Maximum Range:	356MI
Weight:	6,158lbs.
Span:	32FT 8½IN
Length:	29FT 7 1/8IN
Height:	8FT 2½IN
Armament:	One 30MM or Mk 108 engine mounted cannon. Two 13MM MG 131 Cowl mounted machine guns.

49

Special Escort

By the spring of 1944, Allied fighters ranged over Germany and the great slaughter of German fighters began. The heavily armed and armored FW 190A-8/R-8 was the best anti-bomber fighter, but was extremely vulnerable to escorting American fighters. To protect these "bomber killers", new tactics were required. With the advent of the G-10, the fastest G of all, several Reich Defense units formed special staffels. These units were to escort the FW 190s, taking on any Allied fighters and allowing the FW 190s to attack the bombers unmolested. Fw. Horst Petzschler, who flew with JG 54 at this time, has related that he flew a "K type" 109, escorting FW 190s. The unusual thing about this is that all his unit's aircraft were an overall Blue-Grey color, probably Grey 76. This is logical since these aircraft operated at high altitude and the Light Grey color was an effective camouflage.

The photos on this page clearly illustrate this special Grey camouflage. The photo at the lower left is of Werk No. 130368, White 3 of an unknown unit. Note that the fuselage cross is merely a White outline and that the gruppe marking is also White while the swastika is Black. The rudder is not White but merely turned at an angle that reflects light. (Steve Cook Collection)

The photos at the right are of White 43, Werk No. 130369, and White 44, Werk No. 130342 after British markings were added. Both aircraft were of the same unit at Fassburg in 1945.

Interestingly, all these aircraft are the G-10 type with the normal size wheels and wing bulges and long stroke tailwheels.

The Big Blow and Operation Bodenplatte

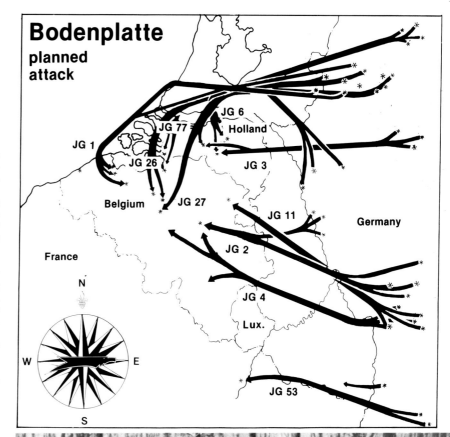

Bodenplatte
planned attack

By the late summer of 1944, the *Luftwaffe* fighter arm had been rendered impotent. Lacking experienced pilots and constantly feeling the pinch of dwindling fuel supplies, units could occassionally inflict heavy casualties on the Allies, but could not influence the course of the airwar. Units were being hammered into oblivion by the merciless harrying of USAAF and RAF fighters. Something sudden and dramatic was needed to alter German fortunes.

Perhaps with rememberances of 1943 in mind, when the Luftwaffe virtually ran the USAAF from German skies, General Adolph Galland decided to conserve his forces. He felt that if he could throw 1500 to 2000 fighters against the USAAF bomber raids, they might destroy 500 bombers. In spite of the anticipated losses of 500 to 600 fighters, the *Jagerstab* though the loss of 500 bombers would stop the USAAF in its tracks.

As the fall wore on and the *Luftwaffe* gathered strength for **"THE BIG BLOW"**, Galland was stunned to receive an order cancelling his operation and ordering his fighters held for a special operation. This, of course, was the December attack through the Ardennes that became known as The Battle of the Bulge. The plan was for the *Jadgeshwadern* to make a tactical attack on the many Allied airfields of the 2nd, 9th and 19th tactical Airforces. The German *Wermacht* staff felt that if surprise were maintained and 1000 Allied fighters were destroyed, considerable paralyzation would talke place keeping the dreaded *Jabos* off the *panzer* spearheads. Galland agreed that this would be useful, but argued that the Allies would quickly replace their aircraft losses, whereas the loss of several hundred bombers in the air would mean the loss of vital crews and this would truely disorganized the Allied airforces. Conversely, German pilots shot down over Allied airfields would be lost, while a considerable number shot down over Germany would survive.

All these arguments fell on deaf ears, however, as nothing was allowed to alter plans for Hitler's last gamble. In the event, the same weather that grounded the Allied airforces, grounded the German units scheduled to take part in *Operation Bodenplatte* as it was now called. Units were equipped with a real managerie of Focke-Wulf 190 and Messerschmitt Bf 109 types. Units participating that used the 109 were *JG 1, JG 2, JG 3, JG 4, JG 6, JG 11, JG 26, JG 27, JG 53 and JG 77*. G-14, G-10 and K-4 types were flown by the various units, frequently types being mixed within *Gruppen*.

The bad weather finally lifted and in spite of the potential element of surprise being lost since the ground attack had already gone in, the signal was given to go ahead with the attack. Traditional New Year's Eve parties were forbidden, much to the disgust of the pilots—in some cases the edict was ignored! The *Geshwaderern* got off at first light on January 1, 1945 and in many cases were led by Ju-88s with navigators to areas close to their targets. However, the secrecy surrounding the operation had precluded notifying the extensive German flak units who presumed that any large formation of aircraft was hostile! As a result, several units were shot at by their own flak and not only took casualties, but suffered disorganization that effected their missions. Some units did not find their assigned targets. The low state of training showed up when repeated straffing runs over several packed Allied airfields resulted in fewer than a dozen Allied losses per field. There was Allied reaction, and Spitfires, Mustangs and Thunderbolts managed to get into action and destroy about 100 of the attackers.

As the Bf 109s straggled back to their airfields there were more losses. Operation Bodenplatte had happened just as Galland had feared. Their accomplishments were less than 200 Allied aircraft destroyed, all of which were replaced within a few days. The last major operation of the Bf 109 had little effect on the war other than to further weaken the *Luftwaffe*.

A G-14, believed to be of JG 53, does an engine warm-up from a dispersed location in the snow. The total domination of Allied airpower in December, 1944 and January 1945 forced the Geshwadern participating in Operation Bodenplatte to hide in locations like this while trying to coordinate deliveries of spares and scarce fuel for the operation. This aircraft has had its landing gear covers removed to prevent clogging by snow.

Bf 109K

The Bf 109K represented another attempt by the all-powerful Fighter Staff to simplify and streamline Bf 109 production. The initial attempt to simplify all the options that were causing confusion and delay in the DB 605A-engined aircraft with the G-14 was reasonably successful. When the more powerful DB 605D was made available, an attempt was made to incorporate all the refinements of the G-14 and G-10 into a single model. The K did this, adding a few refinements of its own.

Externally, the K was similar to the G-10. The wider main wheels and the large rectangular upper wing bulges were made standard. The radio hatch in the left side of the fuselage was relocated forward and higher, the DF loop was moved back a panel, the tailwheel was made retractable with doors, and there were two external trim tabs on the rudder. As far back as the Bf 109F, there were experiments with a wheel well cover and this was finally installed on the K. The wheelwell cover was frequently removed by units in the field, however.

Several versions of the K were planned but there is no evidence to suggest that any of them, other than the K-4 were operational. The K-4 was armed with the deadly 30mm MK 108 cannon firing through the spinner. This weapon had been used sporadically throughout the G series as supplies permitted. It was a remarkable weapon in that 2 or 3 hits was usually sufficient to ensure a kill even on a heavy bomber. The problem with the MK 108 was that it frequently jammed leaving only the 13mm cowl guns and a vulnerable pilot. The problems were ironed out in time for K-4 production and deliveries of this potent warplane began in October, 1944.

Only some 700 K-4 aircraft were produced by April 1945. It served with a variety of units, among them JG 3, JG 4, JG 27, JG 51, JG 52, JG 53 and JG 77.

The K-4 was the apogee of development for the Bf 109. It was a remarkable testimony to the original design and to the tenacity of Messerschmitt's continuing development engineers, that the aircraft was still reasonabley competitive as the war ended. The Luftwaffe had been defeated by a lack of fuel, inept pilot training and overwhelming numbers of enemies. From the beginning to the end, the Messerschmitt Bf 109 was ever willing and able. A truly remarkable machine.

JG 77 was one of the few units to use every variant of the Bf 109G and K. By early spring of 1945 it was not a lack of aircraft or pilots that kept the Luftwaffe on the ground, but an almost total breakdown in fuel supplies. The fuselage sides of White 1 has had an overspray of Grey/Green 02 and spots of Green 82. (Steve Cook Collection)

G-10

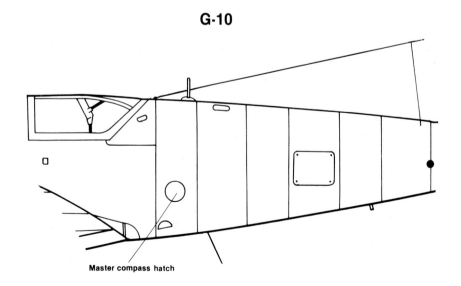

Master compass hatch

K-4

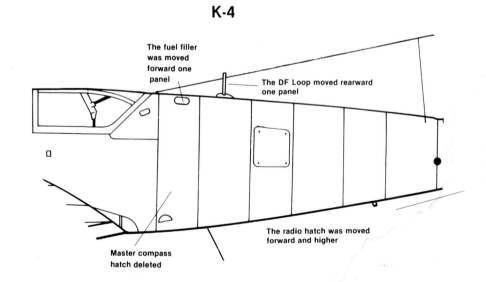

The fuel filler was moved forward one panel

The DF Loop moved rearward one panel

The radio hatch was moved forward and higher

Master compass hatch deleted

The White 17 on this machine, also of I/JG 77, contrasts with the somewhat darker shade of the Balkenkreuz outline, which could be Grey or just plain White that has been exposed to the elements. While the DF loop has been moved rearward, this machine carries an antenna mast. (Steve Cook Collection)

(Above Left) This K-4 of I/JG 77 shows off the big paddle blades that were standard on the K series. The engine mounted 30mm MK 108 cannon firing through the prop hub protruded out of the spinner slightly more than the MG 151/15 or the MG 151/20. (Steve Cook Collection)

Outer Wheel Well Cover

Behind the Gotha Go 145 trainer is a Bf 109K-4. Clearly visible are the outer wheel well covers and the relocated radio hatch, hallmarks of the K-4. (Zdenek Titz)

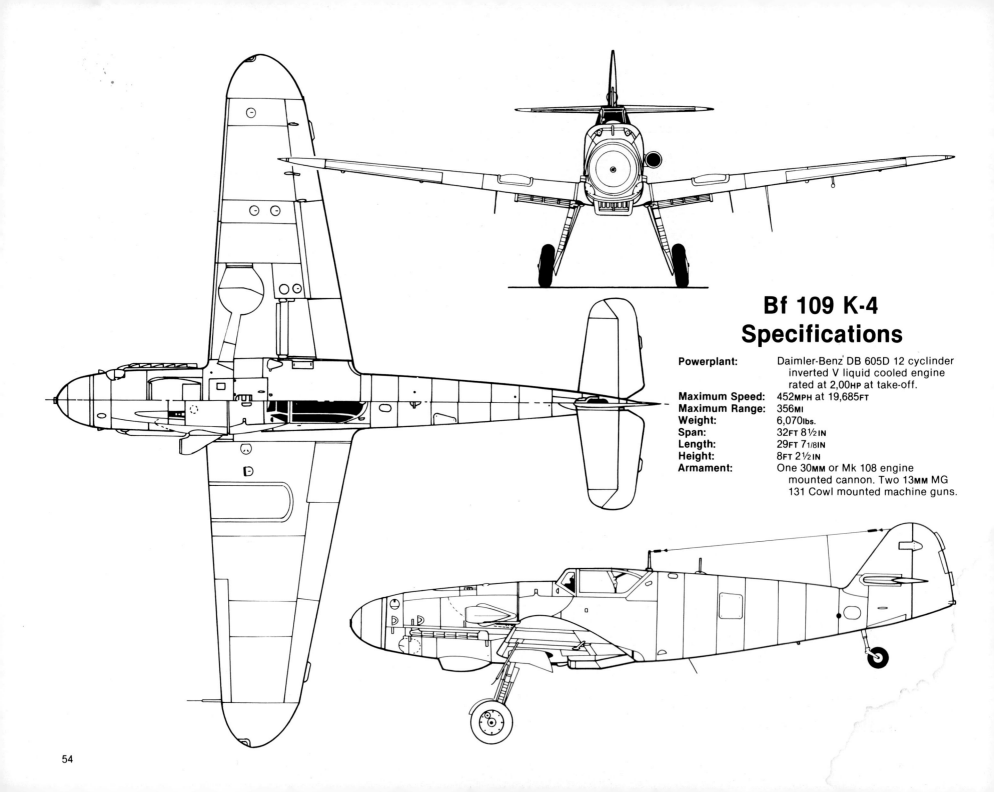

Bf 109 K-4
Specifications

Powerplant: Daimler-Benz DB 605D 12 cyclinder inverted V liquid cooled engine rated at 2,00HP at take-off.
Maximum Speed: 452MPH at 19,685FT
Maximum Range: 356MI
Weight: 6,070lbs.
Span: 32FT 8½IN
Length: 29FT 7 1/8IN
Height: 8FT 2½IN
Armament: One 30MM or Mk 108 engine mounted cannon. Two 13MM MG 131 Cowl mounted machine guns.

K-4 Retractable
Tail Wheel and Doors

Antenna Anchor

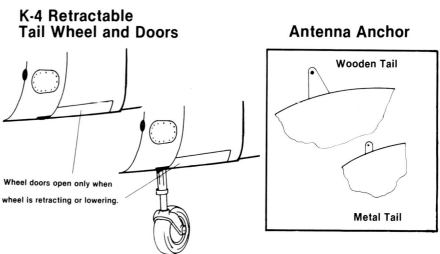

Wheel doors open only when

wheel is retracting or lowering.

Wooden Tail

Metal Tail

These three photographs show a K-4 still in delivery markings after capture by U.S. forces in Amberg, Germany. The black 265 on the rear fuselage are the last three digits of the full Werk No. 334265. By this time in the war, the time-consuming stencil painting of four-digit delivery codes had been abandoned. The camouflage is Olive 81 and Dark Green 82. The main landing gear wheels appear to be unpainted. Unlike almost every 109G and K of this period, the spinner has the old style White quarter instead of the spiral. This aircraft is one of the very few K-4 aircraft fitted with the short fixed tailwheel instead of the long, retractable type. (Steve Cook Collection)

Like JG 77, JG 27 flew almost every 109G type and the K-4. This aircraft, Yellow 1, of III/JG 27 was found abandoned by RAF forces in May of 1945. The wide Green Reich Defense band of JG 27 shows clearly. In the foreground the upper cowling clearly shows the enlarged supercharger intake associated with the DB 605D engine of the K-4. (Steve Cook Collection)

Post-War Developments

The Swiss, in 1944, had agreed to destroy a Bf 110G-4 nightfighter that had landed by accident in Switzerland. The Germans were desperate for this to be done so that its radar secrets would not be learned by the Allies. In exchange for this destruction, the Swiss were allowed to purchase 12 Bf 109G-6 aircraft. These were used in the last years of the war and afterwards. However, the stress of flying and lack of spares took its toll. By 1949, the Swiss Bf 109s were retired.

The end of World War II did not mean the end of service for the Bf 109. The world was a changing place and there was always a need for weapons of whatever type and source.

The Bf 109G-14 had been manufactured in Czechoslovakia until the end of the war. The Czechs found themselves with enough G-14AS components to begin manufacturing under the designation Avia C 10 (service designation S-99). However, only 20 aircraft were produced when the remaining DB 605AS engines were destroyed in a fire. Since the airframes had plenty of life left, the Czechs decided to re-engine them with the Jumo 211F. This resulted in a completely new forward cowling, spinner, and propeller. The resulting aircraft did not handle well in any situation. It was so bad, in fact, that it soon acquired the nickname "mule". Some were sold to Israel's fledgling air force in 1948. Although the aircraft did fly some limited combat, the "mule" proved to be just as unpopular with the Chel Ha'Avir and was quickly phased out of service.

As a wartime ally of the Germans, the Finnish Air Force had received, initially, Bf 109G-2 aircraft and then 109G-6 and a few 109G-8 aircraft. When Finland was forced to accept Soviet terms in the Summer of 1944, the Finnish 109Gs had a kill/loss ration of 12 to 1 which shows what the Gustav could do in the hands of competent pilots. After World War II, the 109G served long and well with the Finns, but lack of spares took its toll and the 109G flew its last mission in 1954. The Finns appreciated the historical importance of the Gustav and two examples have been restored and preserved in Finland today.

The Spanish received 25 G-2 airframes before VE day, but no engines. The assembler first fitted these airframes with the Hispano-Suiza HS 12Z engine. This aircraft was known as the HA-1109-K1L. The HA-1109-K2L and K3L were variants with armament changes. The HA-1110-K1L and HA-1112-K1L were two-place trainers of which only a few examples were built. This mating was less than satisfactory, so experiments soon began using the Rolls-Royce Merlin engine.

Various 1109-K1L, K2L and K3L aircraft served as prototypes for this Merlin version. Use of the Merlin meant no engine armament. The production version was known as the HA-1112-M1L. A two-place trainer with the tall wooden tail was known as the HA-1112-M4L. These aircraft were retired in 1967 and several were bought for the film, THE BATTLE OF BRITAIN. These aircraft are now in various private collections including the Confederate Air Force in Texas.

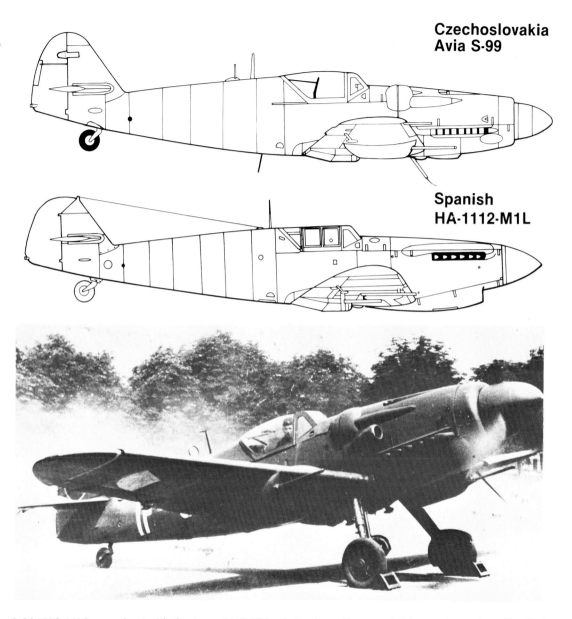

A Bf 109G-14AS re-engined with the Jumo 211F. This photo shows the completely new forward cowling that resulted from this mating. This aircraft having a ground test run-up, also exhibits other changes: the spinner, relocated DF loop and radio antenna, and the new main canopy with a "blown" shape and new pilot armor plate. The aircraft also carries the 20mm underwing cannon, wide main wheels and fuselage rack for a 250kg bomb. These aircraft were an overall Olive Green with Czech. national insignia in six positions. This aircraft has the White codes IF-01. (Frantizek Sazel)